DIVORCE HANGOVER

Do you . . .

Think obsessiv[...]

Have revenge fa[...]

Try to seduce your ex when he comes to pick up the kids?

Send the child support check late every month?

Punish your ex by not packing the kids' clothes for the weekend? Or by refusing to pay for their school supplies?

Constantly bad-mouth your ex's new mate to the children?

Believe that all men are a waste of time? Or that all women are gold diggers?

Live through your children now that your spouse is gone?

If so, you are suffering from a DIVORCE HANGOVER that can adversely affect not only your life, but the lives of everyone around you: children, ex-spouses, friends, co-workers, family—and, if you're not careful, your *new* mate. With the help of the exercises and workbooks in this unique step-by-step guide, you'll learn to break free from destructive patterns of post-divorce dependence, turn negative attitudes into positive ones, and create a bright future for yourself and for the people you love most.

DIVORCE HANGOVER

ANNE N. WALTHER, M.S.

POCKET BOOKS

New York   London   Toronto   Sydney   Tokyo   Singapore

POCKET BOOKS, a division of Simon & Schuster Inc.
1230 Avenue of the Americas, New York, NY 10020

ISBN: 0-671-70332-3

First Pocket Books paperback printing April 1992

10 9 8 7 6 5 4 3 2

POCKET and colophon are registered trademarks of
Simon & Schuster Inc.

Cover photo by Bill Westheimer

Printed in the U.S.A.

To Roger, *my new mate of fifteen years,
who proves that there is life and love
after divorce.*

◆

*And to Paula, without whose
encouragement and support this
manuscript would never have made the
drawing board.*

Acknowledgments

The life of this book has been a tapestry of both friends and professionals who have contributed a myriad of colors and textures to the final cloth. I would particularly like to thank my editor, Judith Regan, and my agent, Maria Theresa Caen—and my very special appreciation to Carol Costello, a master tailor and seamstress.

Contents

◆ II ◆

Managing Your World and Keeping the Hangover at Bay

Epilogue

Preface

One out of every two marriages ends in divorce, but we have not yet learned to end marriages in ways that heal us emotionally and put closure on that part of our lives.

Some pain, anxiety, anger, or depression is inevitable after a divorce, but when these feelings persist, they turn into what I call the divorce hangover—a crippling condition that keeps you from living life fully in the present and moving forward into the future.

This book presents some practical strategies for healing the divorce hangover so that you can:

- Pull yourself out of the emotional quicksand of a limiting or painful connection to your ex-spouse and former life
- Release the anger, resentment, and confusion
- Replace self-destructive attitudes and behaviors with positive ones and rebuild self-esteem
- Take back control of your life
- Move into a future that you create and design

If you are in the process of divorcing, this book can help you avoid the hangover altogether.

For women especially, the reality of divorce can be very daunting. Statistics reveal that the majority of women with children experience a drop in their standard of living following a divorce and almost half receive no child support at all. In my work as a career counselor, I've found that a person's difficulties with work or career often have their roots in a divorce hangover. When the pain, confusion, and anger of the hangover are healed, professional and financial problems are resolved more easily. This is true for *both* men and women.

You may recognize your story in this book. Though each

person's situation is unique, we all share certain universal experiences in a divorce or divorce hangover. Remember, *you are not alone*.

And believe it or not, congratulations are in order. In deciding to heal your divorce hangover, you have made a courageous commitment to yourself and your future. That is the first step, and the most important one.

UNDERSTANDING AND HEALING A DIVORCE HANGOVER

◇

• 1 •

Do You Have a Divorce Hangover?

◇

What we do not understand we cannot control.

—CHARLES REICH

◇

Divorce is a profound, life-changing experience. It is painful, it is confusing, and it turns your world upside down. But at some point, it should be *over*.

If it's not, if the pain, anger, resentment, depression, or emotional confusion seem to go on forever, then you are in the clutches of a divorce hangover. A hangover is an ongoing connection with your ex-spouse or former life that keeps you agitated or depressed, unhappy, and stuck in the past.

You deserve to come to peace with your divorce so that you can begin a new and richer life. To do that, you must first understand the divorce hangover.

Pain That Won't Stop

Jan thought her divorce was over when the judge's gavel swung down and the decree was final, but months later she was still crying herself to sleep.

She thought the pain and frustration would end when she received the financial settlement, but she still caught herself lashing out for no apparent reason at the children and strangers. There were days when her emotions, her finances, and her life seemed completely out of control.

Later, she thought the anger and resentment would finally end when she moved to a new city . . . when she began seeing someone and remarried . . . when her ex-husband, Tom, remarried and had a child.

But the knot in her stomach still hasn't gone away, even after eight years. She still finds herself replaying the marriage and divorce over and over in her mind, and often feels angry, depressed, or victimized when she thinks about Tom. Sometimes it doesn't take much to set her off—a wedding invitation, parents' night at the kids' school, a Fourth of July picnic, anything that reminds her of all that she has lost.

For Jan, the emotional loose ends and unresolved bad feelings have become a habit. Ever since the divorce, she feels as if she's living at only half speed, or underwater. Her feelings about Tom and the divorce still control her life. So much of her attention and energy are focused on the past—which she can do nothing to change—that she sees even her new marriage to John through the filter of this "failure."

Jan's "hangover" has little to do with external events like signing the final papers or starting to see other people. Rather, it is an internal state of mind that she carries with her everywhere as a shield against the loss, change, pain, and devastation of her divorce—and the fear that something even worse could happen in the future. This shield, which is keeping her from moving forward with her life, is a divorce hangover.

And Jan is not alone.

Some Hangover Scenarios

Does any of these situations sound familiar?

- Seven years after the divorce, Fran calls her ex-husband's new wife, Isabella, and shrieks into the phone, "Give me my husband, you bitch!" Robert, now Isabella's husband, passively sits by, refusing to get an unlisted phone number, thereby causing a rift in his present marriage.
- George has been divorced for three years and is happily remarried, but he continues to pay for his first wife's subscription to *TV Guide*.
- Stacy continues to drive the old Mustang that she and Rick shared when they were married, even though she can afford a new car. Each time it breaks down, she calls Rick immediately, convinced that he is the only one who can fix it.
- Jennifer, 10, tells her mother "all kinds of things" after weekends with her father, particularly about his "rotten new girlfriend." She will do anything to keep her divorced parents "together," even if their only connection is arguing on the phone.
- Two years after his divorce, Ed is still living in the same small apartment, complaining about the unfair financial settlement. He bitterly claims he doesn't have enough money to date and spends his energy bad-mouthing his ex to anyone who'll listen.
- Bob's suits are still hanging in Alice's closet, even though his new wife just gave birth to their second child.
- Allen's ex-wife, Judy, has been living with her boyfriend ever since their divorce four years ago, but he still thinks she will one day come back to him.
- Mary "accidentally" packs dirty clothes for the children's weekends with Dan, remembering how much he always hated to do the laundry.
- Bart is convinced that the only reason his ex-wife isn't

marrying her "live-in" is that it would end his alimony payments to her.

Fifty percent of all American marriages end in divorce. How can something that happens that often be so confusing and so painful? And how can it last so long?

While the *legal process* of divorce is fairly simple—one entity is divided into two separate entities—the *emotional experience* of divorce can be complex and devastating. When a divorce does not promote healing and lay the past to rest, you feel the pain and paralysis of a divorce hangover. Divorce hangover is the *unfinished* emotional experience of the divorce.

But that hangover can be healed. Divorce does not have to be a permanent state of being, a condition that keeps you trapped in chronic pain or numbness. It is the end of one phase of your life, and regardless of whether it was by choice or not, it can be the beginning of a happier, more satisfying one.

Ties That Bind

Recognizing your hangover is the first step toward healing the pain. You are in the grip of the divorce hangover if:

- *You still have strong emotional ties to your ex-spouse.* These ties may be negative—a confusing, chaotic storm of anger, depression, bitterness, fear, resentment, guilt, blame, anxiety, or frustration—but they still keep you connected.

  You get upset when you think of your ex-spouse or hear his or her name, even bursting into tears if something reminds you of that person. You think about what you could do to *get back* at the other person, or what you could do to get him or her *back*.

- *Your energy is galvanized by these feelings;* sometimes they are the only things that get you going or keep you going.

- *You feel victimized* by your ex-spouse, the lawyers, or the divorce in general. You want your ex-spouse to be punished, to suffer for all he or she has done to you . . . or you just want to crawl under a rock, letting the world go on without you.

- *You think obsessively about your ex-spouse.* You wonder who he or she is seeing; what sex is like with that new partner; how your ex-spouse looks now; what he or she would think of the person *you're* seeing; what it would be like if you got back together; and whether there was something you could have done to avoid the divorce . . . or you look back in anger, preoccupied with what your ex-spouse did to you or what you're going to do to him or her.
- *You see him or her more often than necessary.* You could have called a plumber to fix the faucet, a decorator to arrange the living room furniture, your mother for a recipe, or a financial advisor about buying this or that stock—but you didn't. Instead, you called your ex-spouse. You could have handled that matter with the kids or the finances over the phone, but instead you met for cocktails.
- *The past seems more real to you than the present.*
- *You still feel as if your life is on hold.*

These feelings can be conscious or unconscious, explosive or subtle. If they focus your attention and energy on the past, or if they make you angry, anxious, depressed, or wistful about what might have been, then they are not healthy. As long as you are still emotionally *engaged* and *entangled* with your ex-spouse in these ways, you can't live in the present or move forward into the future.

The divorce hangover does not discriminate. It can affect anyone, regardless of sex, social or financial status, or even who initiated the divorce.

And it doesn't matter how long ago your divorce happened. If you still think about it or about your ex-spouse in emotionally charged ways, if your fists clench or your body tightens when you hear his or her name, if that former life is as real to you as your present life, then it's time to stop and take stock of where you are.

Variations on a Theme

There are as many varieties of hangovers as there are divorced people.

Steamy: Jean and Tom's relationship was always passionate, and they brought into the divorce not only their violent arguments but their strong sexual attraction.

When he comes to pick up the children, it's not unusual for her to be dressed seductively and invite him upstairs to see or fix something. Sometimes these encounters explode into shouting matches, but just as often the children are invited to play with the neighbor kids for a while before Tom takes them for the weekend.

Violent: Burt and Melanie had a different dynamic. Burt became involved with his present wife before he and Melanie were divorced, and Melanie has never gotten over it.

She tried to punish him with a brutal financial settlement, and when that was over, she began writing abusive letters to him and phoning his new wife at work, calling her a whore. Finally, she started following the new wife around and once even attacked her, causing physical harm. Melanie's entire life was consumed by her obsession with blaming and destroying Burt's new wife.

Morose: Bonnie hasn't seen Arnold in the six years since her divorce was final, but she has thought of little else. She's consumed with what he is doing in his spare time, whom he is seeing, how much money he makes now, what his apartment looks like . . . and she is very clever about obtaining information from mutual friends.

Sometimes she feels furious and wants to punish him for

leaving her; other times, she cries because they are no longer together. She sees her whole life in terms of her divorce. She is a divorced woman. Arnold is her ex-husband. A friend's wedding means a potential divorce. Children are something she and Arnold didn't have.

Her friends have started to fall away because she is at best, wistful; at worst, bitter. They don't want to be around someone who clings so desperately to the past.

Numbing: Elaine appears fine but she's really in a mild depression. She gets the kids off to school, goes to work, manages the stress of single parenting fairly well, and earns enough money so their lifestyle has changed only slightly. But since the divorce four years ago, she hasn't been attracted to anyone romantically, has let many of her friendships lag, and has lost interest in activities like singing, jogging, and the gourmet cooking group she started.

She feels she is only part of the person she was when she was married. At 36, she chalks this up to getting old.

Time Bomb

The divorce hangover has a way of surfacing at the most inappropriate and inconvenient times. It can strike out at the driver in the next lane, the neighbor's dog, co-workers, demanding children, and oversolicitous friends.

When you have a divorce hangover, life is a battlefield, and unfortunately, you and the people in your life are often the worst casualties. Anger, resentment, bitterness, depression, and frustration can also cause physical illness if you keep them around for long periods of time. Ultimately, you only hurt yourself with vengeful or bitter thoughts and actions.

Paul almost let his hangover ruin the successful computer business he had started twenty years ago. Before his divorce he genuinely cared about the people who worked for him and seemed to bring out the best in everyone. He was able to draw the most competent and creative people in the field.

After his divorce, Paul began to find fault with people's work. He seemed withdrawn, and people began to pull back from him. The more he demanded, the less they seemed to produce. The product became secondary to ugly office politics, and the company lost the family atmosphere that had contributed so strongly to its success. Paul had always loved going into the office; now it seemed like a nightmare.

When he came to me for career counseling, Paul was ready to sell his company and go to work for a larger corporation because he needed something more *secure*. By talking about his divorce he began to see that perhaps his desire for more security in his job was a reaction to the insecurity he now felt in his personal life.

He also realized that the easy camaraderie with his employees was gone largely because he felt too vulnerable to be available to them on a personal level. This revelation enabled him to try to open up more at work, and eventually, he was again able to run his company successfully and in a way that met his needs.

The divorce hangover time bomb might have blown up in his face, but he defused it by understanding how it worked and by making changes.

• 2 •

What Does Your Hangover Look Like?

◇

All thoughts of a turtle are turtles,
And of a rabbit, rabbits.
　　　　　　—RALPH WALDO EMERSON
　　　　　　NATURAL HISTORY OF THE INTELLECT

◇

15 Symptoms

When you hear the words *divorce hangover*, you may know instinctively if you are involved in one. But to really understand, look for these specific symptoms:

1. *Sarcasm:* When someone mentions your ex-spouse, you tend to be sarcastic or take potshots. Your sarcasm extends to all relationships in general or to marriage in particular, resulting in comments like, "All men leave their wives the minute they turn forty" or "All women are just after my money."

2. *Using the children:* You want to make sure the children understand that nothing about the divorce was *your* fault, so you make it all your ex-spouse's fault.

11

You also prod them for information about their other parent.

3. *Lashing out:* You feel so helpless that often you lash out or try to assert control in inappropriate ways in an effort to prove to yourself and to your ex-spouse that you have some power in this situation.

   You may make extraordinary demands—wanting the children all weekend, every weekend, or else making it hard for the other parent to see them at all. You may drag the other person back to court for a better financial settlement when you don't really need the money. You may blow up at a friend because he or she went to a party at your ex-spouse's house. These efforts usually backfire, however, and only create more bitterness, resentment, and crossfire. In fact, they undercut what power you do have.

4. *Not feeling:* You feel emotionally "flat"—never particularly upset, or particularly happy, about anything. You repress your emotional responses in an effort not to feel the pain.

5. *Paralysis:* You can't seem to do the things you know you should do or want to do: start back to school, get a new job, become involved in a new relationship, find new interests. Sometimes it's even hard to clean the house, get up in the morning and go to work, call a friend, or go out to a movie. You just can't seem to take the first step, and then beat yourself up for staying stuck.

6. *Holding on:* You may literally hold on to things: furniture, an 8×10 photograph of your ex-spouse that still sits on the piano a year after your divorce, his or her old clothing, anything that keeps the other person's presence alive in your daily life.

7. *Throwing out the baby with the bathwater:* On the other hand, you may throw away things of value, simply because they remind you of your ex-spouse. This suggests just as much attachment as holding on. It doesn't make sense to toss out priceless jewelry, art, or

anything valuable just to make a statement, to get back at him or her, or to do something dramatic.

8. *Self-fulfilling prophecies and catastrophic expectations:* Fearful, angry thoughts and predictions build a mass of negativity—and these statements may actually start coming true. "The children will be ruined by this." "This party is going to be awful." "He'll just be after one thing." "She's going to set me up and then leave." You anticipate the worst in an attempt never to be taken off guard again.

9. *Unrealistic expectations:* You never want to deal with pain again, so next time everything had better be perfect. "I won't go out with him unless he's sexy, wealthy, a Ph.D., and thinks I walk on water." "She'd better be beautiful, understanding, great in bed, and self-sufficient."

10. *Blaming and finding fault:* You believe that some or all of what went wrong in the marriage or the divorce was someone else's fault—your ex-spouse, his or her mother, his or her lover, his or her kids, his or her ex-spouse, his or her job, his or her golf game, etc.

11. *Excessive guilt:* You believe you are at fault because the marriage failed whether you did the leaving or not. You buy your kids whatever they want, and give in to their or your ex-spouse's demands, however unreasonable.

12. *Self-pity or feeling victimized:* It's natural to feel sorry for yourself after losing a marriage, but self-pity can become a habit when it is indulged. "I've lost everything and I'll never be happy again." "I'm too old to start over now." This places you in the role of victim, which is a "no win" place to be.

13. *Running away:* You may need some time away from the "scene of the crime," but you can't stay at the beach or in the mountains forever. At some point, you have to come home, face the music, and start rebuilding. No matter how fast or far you run, you can't leave your feelings behind.

14. *Living vicariously:* When you use other people's per-

sonalities, abilities, achievements, and activities to define yourself, you miss out on living your own life. After a divorce, there is a particular tendency to want to live through the children. They may represent the best of the marriage and they are often close by, at least emotionally. It's natural to want to use them to avoid dealing with yourself—but this isn't fair to them or healthy for you.

15. *Dependency:* You lean on other people, particularly new romantic involvements, to help define who you are in this new time. Complete isolation isn't usually healthy, but it is important to take some time to ponder "Who am I now?" without anyone else waiting or watching for the answer. A healthy attitude in this area is: "I am whole without a mate or a significant other." An unhealthy, dependent attitude is: "I am only half a person if I am not in a relationship."

The Divorce Hangover Paradox

Nobody sets out to acquire a divorce hangover, and having one doesn't make you a bad person. It's something that sneaks up on you when you are vulnerable, a natural response to the pain and loss of divorce. Once it's in place, it becomes a habit.

The problem is that the divorce hangover does *not* protect you from the pain; it only makes the pain worse and keeps you from working through the anger and confusion. Without the hangover "protecting" and binding you, you could face up to the loss, move through pain, and sever the self-destructive emotional ties with your ex-spouse.

• 3 •

What Does the Divorce
Hangover Cost You?

◇

What other dungeon is so dark
As one of one's own making.
What jailor so inexorable as one's self!
—NATHANIEL HAWTHORNE,
THE HOUSE OF SEVEN GABLES

◇

The emotional toll of a hangover is so enormous that it's hard to calculate. It saps your energy, creates walls between you and other people, and keeps you in a state of constant pain, agitation, or depression. It's like holding your hand in water long after you realize that it is too hot.

The hangover can deprive you of happiness, self-esteem, future relationships, money, professional success, friends, the love and respect of your children, and whatever else you hold dear. Some crucial areas of deprivation are:

- *Sex:* Sex may lose its appeal, or take on elements of anger or fear, if it was used as a weapon in the marriage or divorce—or if you simply associate it strongly or exclusively with your ex-spouse.

- *Trust:* After being "betrayed" by a spouse who has left or feeling betrayed by a marriage that couldn't work, your ability to trust may be seriously hampered.
- *Energy:* You can spend every waking moment plotting revenge for what your ex-spouse did to you, worrying about what he or she will do next, or agonizing over your future, leaving you less time and energy for managing your day-to-day *real* life.
- *Health:* Your unresolved emotions and your stress turn inward, causing migraines, stomach troubles, or a host of other ailments and illnesses.

You know better than anyone what the divorce hangover costs you and what you sacrifice to keep it around.

Healing: What's in It for You?

You may have guessed already that to cure the hangover, you'll have to go back and face some old pains. Why should you do that? Why drag up the past? Why not leave well enough alone? Won't time heal all?

Unfortunately, this isn't the type of hangover that goes away with a couple of aspirin and a good night's sleep. The longer you let it continue, the worse it gets. Eventually, it can become the whole focus of your life.

You will discover your own best reasons for giving up the divorce hangover, but here are six good ones:

- *You stop hurting.* The pain of a divorce hangover goes on forever, unless you heal it. This healing process isn't comfortable, but at some point, the pain is over and you are free.
- *You get on with your life.* You are no longer captive to the gnawing pain, limiting attitudes, and restrictive be-

haviors of the divorce hangover. Instead of hanging suspended somewhere between the marriage and the divorce, you take a stand for the future.

• *You wake up.* Instead of withdrawing from life for fear of what *else* might happen, you take off the blinders and begin seeing the personal and professional opportunities that are all around you. If you pass the love of your life on the street, you will actually see him or her. If a chance to develop your career hits you over the head, you will feel it.

• *You grow in positive ways.* You can't keep a living organism from growing. Plants will creep around rocks and even grow through windows. They will bend or twist if they have to—but they *will grow.* Healing the divorce hangover lets you grow strong and straight.

• *You find peace.* Unless you let go, life remains a minefield, a series of triggers that can catapult you without warning into what I call "the whirlies," a maelstrom of unreasonable anger, depression, and emotional chaos.

• *You find new people and have more fulfilling relationships.* Healing does not guarantee that you will fall in love within a week, but it does open you to new people and new possibilities. You are also less likely to repeat old mistakes. The attitudes you develop and the skills you learn in healing a divorce hangover can enrich your relationships with children, family, friends, and future mate.

There is no longer any need to endure the burden of your divorce hangover. You deserve to wake up each morning feeling relaxed, happy, and ready to embrace the day.

Your Workbook

The workbook part of this book is very important.

At the end of each chapter, there will be exercises to help you apply what you have just read to your own special circumstances.

Sometimes people nod and look blank when I talk about the workbook, and I know they're thinking: "I'll do the exercises in my mind; I don't have to write this stuff down."

But I urge you, even if you have an aversion to writing, do make the effort to do this. There is a power in writing things down, as you will soon find out.

Your workbook is for your eyes only so that you may write whatever you want without fear that anyone will see it. You need a safe place to say *anything* without censoring or fearing being judged—even by your own critical mind. The only rule about the workbook is that there is no getting down on yourself for anything you write in it.

Your workbook will also help when you feel confused or out of control. You can go back and look at what you wrote, to remember what you really think and feel, or to work through whatever is bothering you. People have told me that the workbook is their lifeline. It's the way they pull themselves out of their emotional turmoil and start to make decisions, how they move from feeling helpless to feeling powerful.

So, have fun with this, buy a notebook—spiral, loose-leaf, diary, or whatever appeals to you—and use it for just this purpose. Choose a color or style you like, and perhaps even a pen with an unusual color ink. You deserve the time, energy, and attention it takes to work through your divorce hangover.

Doing the Exercises

Some people get into the old "school mode" and race through the exercises as if it mattered who finished first. Take your time. Think about your answers. They will become the basis for your new life, and that deserves respect.

Before you begin each workbook section, take a moment to relax. Take some deep breaths, do some stretches, do whatever helps you to relax and think clearly.

You may want to use a guided relaxation exercise such as this each time you begin a set of workbook questions: Sit back and close your eyes. Take a deep breath and slowly let it out. Now take several more deep breaths. As you let each breath out, feel the tension flow out of your body. Visualize a quiet place with green grass and a peaceful lake. Hear the gentle lapping of the water on the shore. Feel a soft breeze against your face, and the warmth of the sun. Continue to breathe deeply. Each time you exhale, notice that you are feeling more tranquil and at peace. When you are ready, slowly open your eyes and begin.

Any peaceful or beautiful image can be recreated in your visualization.

SUMMARY

- The divorce hangover is a network of strong emotions that keep you connected to your ex-spouse and stuck in the past.

- Divorce hangover behaviors are:
  —Thinking obsessively about your ex-spouse
  —Emotional reactions to your ex-spouse
  —Relying on your ex-spouse more than necessary

- The divorce hangover costs:
  —Time
  —Money
  —Relationships
  —Emotional and physical energy

- Knowing what your hangover looks like helps you avoid hangover behaviors.

◆
WORKBOOK EXERCISES
◆

Enter these questions in your workbook, and take your time answering them. The more thoroughly you answer each question, the more information you will get about yourself and your hangover.

1. Think about something your ex-spouse did or said that made you angry. What are your physical and emotional reactions to this memory? After taking a moment to rest and relax again, recreate the same scene in your mind. This time, substitute a good friend for your ex-spouse. If you don't have the same physical reactions or feelings when your friend does or says the same things, then you have a divorce hangover.

2. Think of other negative encounters between you and your ex-spouse. Write them down and be as specific as possible. These are the issues of your divorce hangover.

3. List the ties you still have with your ex-spouse (emotional, financial, children, etc.).

4. Do you get a negative or positive emotional payoff from these connections? Describe.

5. Go down the following list, putting the appropriate name (yours, your ex-spouse's, or both) next to the symptoms that the person has shown:
   • being sarcastic
   • using the children
   • lashing out
   • suppressing feelings
   • acting paralyzed
   • holding on

- throwing the baby out with the bathwater
- making self-fulfilling prophecies
- having unrealistic expectations
- blaming
- having excessive guilt
- feeling victimized
- escaping
- living vicariously
- being overly dependent.

Give an example of each.

6. How much time do you devote to negative feelings and behaviors concerning your ex-spouse and your divorce?

7. What has been the emotional cost to you of the divorce hangover? The physical cost? The financial cost? The relationship cost?

• 4 •

10 Steps to Healing
the Hangover

◇

The secret of walking on water is knowing
where the stones are.

—ANONYMOUS

◇

You can cure the divorce hangover using the ten practical steps presented in this chapter. It may take some patience and attention, but the most important ingredient is your own desire to be free of the hangover.

Everyone experiencing divorce is held in a maze of devastating emotions. The one that seems to be the most shattering and the hardest to endure is loneliness. The fear of being alone has held many in intolerable marriages. Recently, a friend of mine was describing her fiftieth wedding anniversary. She said that during the evening her children openly spoke of their amazement that their parents had stayed married. My friend wasn't surprised at their amazement. "The only thing that kept me in that marriage was that every time I thought of divorce, the thought of the loneliness was so overwhelming to me that I simply could not consider it."

Friends and clients alike speak of the loneliness of divorce and afterward. "I have been divorced 15 years," one said. "The pain is as sharp and exhausting today as it was the moment the whole thing began. Maybe even more so." In order to escape, anything is preferable—running to relationships, bad or good; alcohol; drugs; work—to numb the pain. No one seems immune, and I was no exception. I handled the days fairly well. I used the needs of the children, work, and the house to distract me from the gnawing feeling in the pit of my stomach. But night was the enemy. The house was quiet and there I was with myself, alone. I felt trapped in a web of fear, anger, anxiety, confusion, insecurity, frustration, and loneliness. It was like walking through emotional quicksand. I couldn't move, couldn't stand still, couldn't get anything done, couldn't make sense of things, and kept asking myself, "What's wrong with me?"

I was trying to be *more* capable and competent during that time; instead, I felt *less* so. Each time I thought I had things under control, a new piece of the chaos would spring up and I'd start struggling again, feeling disoriented and out of control. It seemed as if the emotional roller coaster would never end.

I knew the answer was to get a grip on my emotions and to start making rational decisions, but that seemed impossible until I untangled myself from the emotional turmoil.

STEP **1**   ◇   ◇   ◇   ◇   ◇   ◇

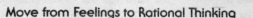

Move from Feelings to Rational Thinking

It's a vicious circle. As long as you are in an emotional tailspin, you are motivated by fear—and fear feeds the tailspin. Before you can do anything else, you have to stop that downward spiral.

It all came to a head for Diane one rainy morning as she was getting the kids, ages 6 and 8, off to school. "Megan had a cold and probably shouldn't even have been going to school that day, but it was too late to get a sitter and I couldn't take another day off work. Robbie wanted me to check his math, but if I did we'd *all* be late. I'd dropped the mayo when I was making their sandwiches and was trying to keep the dog out of the glass and goop on the kitchen floor, everybody was screaming, I wasn't being a good mother, and then I looked up and saw the school bus pulling away without my kids. Now I had to drop them off, and my boss would yell at me for being late again. I just lost it. I sat down and sobbed, which made things even worse for them. I never planned to raise and support two children by myself. I never signed on for this. . . ."

It's hard even to do grocery shopping or walk across the street when you're in an emotional tailspin. You're at the end of your rope. One more question from the kids, one more bill in the mail, one more harsh word from your boss, one more "chance meeting" with your ex-spouse's new partner, and you're going to lose it.

THE WAY OUT

Tailspins don't stop by themselves; you have to pull yourself out of them. At some point, you have to reach out and consciously begin to manage your emotions. This will become easier to do as you read this book and begin to understand how the hangover starts, what keeps it in place, what yours looks like, what it's protecting you from, and how you can release it.

The minute you start to consider those answers, you begin a *mental* process that pulls you out of the *emotional freefall*. At this point, you start to take charge.

Moving from feelings *to* rational thinking *is the way to stop the emotional tailspin*. If you can think about something, you can put it outside of yourself. You may still *have* some of those feelings, but they don't have *you*.

That rainy morning, as Diane sobbed, her despairing thoughts began to take over. As she looked up through her tears, she saw her children's frightened faces and knew she had to pull it together. Quickly she asked herself, "What am I feeling?" Overwhelmed, was the first thought, but also scared and sick of it all. Why couldn't someone take care of her? She had managed many other mornings since the divorce and most of the time she did a great job. No, her thoughts continued, I won't lose my job if I miss work today, and certainly not if I get there a bit late. Megan has no fever and I can drive the kids to school and take the time to clean this mess. This is a *tough* morning and I deserve the time to make it more manageable.

Diane allowed her emotions to surface and be identified and accepted them without self-pity, blame, or other judgment. She was then able to make rational decisions and move into action.

Actually, Diane solved her morning crisis by using a combination of rational steps; but without taking the first—that is, making a conscious decision to think and act rather than feel and react—the rest of the crisis-solving process could not have taken place.

◆

SUMMARY

- The emotional tailspin of a divorce hangover is fueled by feelings of anger, depression, confusion, and loss of control.

- The key to pulling out of a tailspin is moving from the *emotional* to the *rational*.

◆

◆

WORKBOOK EXERCISES
◆

1. At the time of the divorce, which feelings hit you the hardest? Rank the following: anger, depression, anxiety, tiredness, fear, loss, helplessness, aloneness, bitterness, vindictiveness, feeling exploited, others.

2. What are your feelings now?

3. What caused and continues to cause these feelings?

4. What can you do about each of these feelings?

STEP **2** ◇   ◇   ◇   ◇   ◇   ◇

Answer the Key Questions

If you are in the process of a divorce now, these questions will be the basis for all your other decisions and help you avoid a hangover. If you are healing a hangover, they will help you clarify what really happened in your marriage and divorce, why it happened, how your hangover developed, and what you can do about it now.

THE KEY QUESTIONS

1. Was your divorce inevitable?
2. What was the cause of your divorce?
3. What were your expectations going into the marriage?
4. How long did you want it to take to get the divorce?

5. What was your first priority in the divorce?
6. What was the greatest benefit to you?

Exploring these questions will show how the decisions you made—or did *not* make—at the time of your divorce affected your hangover. As you answer these questions, you will begin to see exactly how your hangover took shape.

1. Was your divorce inevitable?

This is the first question you should ask, and may be the most important. Not asking it is a primary cause of the confusion surrounding divorce.

If you decide that your divorce was inevitable, then at least you know that you are in the right place. You can put to rest forever all the doubts, worries, fears, and second-guessing about whether you did the right thing. You did! There was never really an alternative.

This seems like an obvious question, but I know some very bright men and women who never asked it and spent the next twenty years wondering:

- "If I'd given in on that one issue, would we still be together?"
- "If he'd just stopped drinking, would the kids have had a father over those important years?"
- "Maybe if we'd seen a therapist, or if I'd just overlooked those two affairs . . . we might be happy today."

This kind of backward, "coulda, woulda, shoulda" thinking keeps you trapped in the past. It can also keep you trapped in the present when it's time to move on. In deciding whether or not to stay in a relationship, I've heard equally bright men and women say things like:

- "He just drinks because he doesn't know what it is to be really loved. I'll show him, and then things will be better."
- "I'm sure once we're married awhile, she'll change her mind and want to have kids."

- "If I'm patient with him, he'll open up to me emotionally."

These people were all walking into a trap, *the false hope that maybe the other person would change*. None of us would be divorced if it were possible to change other people into who we think they should be. Thinking that the other person will change is like dropping a pencil and expecting it to fall up instead of down. Things just don't work that way. Rather than thinking about how things *might* have worked out, the question to ask is: *"If the other person had never changed—and if I had never changed—would I still have wanted to stay in that relationship?"*

As you were then, and as the other person was then, would it have worked? Answering this question eliminates all the false hopes, the self-delusions, the "what if's," the "maybe if he or she, then I's," and the "maybe if I, then he or she's."

Notice that the question is not "Did you *want* your divorce?" but "Was your divorce inevitable?" You know the answer. Face it head on. If the other person wanted to leave, and especially if there was a third party involved, it probably was inevitable. If your ex-spouse was involved in something you couldn't live with—alcoholism, compulsive spending, etc.—you may not have *wanted* the divorce, but it may have been the only real choice between two evils.

If your divorce was final years ago and there has been no reconciliation, then obviously it has turned out to be inevitable and you must treat it as such.

Some people avoid asking this question because they want to be able to say later, "Well, I never wanted the divorce." But refusing any responsibility for choosing or accepting it keeps one stuck in the role of the victim who may never be able to take hold of his or her life.

The inevitability of the divorce is your take-off point, the basic piece of information to which you can always return when you feel yourself waffling. Eventually you must come to feel there was nothing you could have done then, and there is nothing you can do now to bring that marriage back. You must believe that any effort in that direction is a waste of time. Then you will see that the only direction to look now is ahead.

2. What was the cause of your divorce?

Some of the most common reasons people give for divorce are drug or alcohol abuse, sexual differences or preferences, infidelity, physical violence, difficulties with the balance of power, money problems, children, and in-laws.

But other, more subtle reasons have surfaced only in the past thirty years or so, as personal growth and fulfilling relationships have become more important in our culture. Today, we are less willing to tolerate stagnant or psychologically destructive marriages.

Unmet Expectations: Saying you want a divorce because of "unmet expectations" may not be given much credence. You may feel you have to justify divorce—to yourself and other people—if the marriage simply didn't turn out the way you expected it would.

It's often hard even to say exactly what we mean by "unmet expectations." You may wake up one morning and realize that there is nothing there. You may feel you are in a cage and the walls are closing in. This situation can be psychologically punishing, and in many ways as damaging as being physically abused, *even if it appears that the other person isn't doing any intentional or tangible harm.*

We are much more alert and sensitive to these kinds of issues today than we used to be. Before the revelations and revolutions of the 1960's, people were more inclined to stay married and turn to affairs, drugs or alcohol, prolonged absences, or whatever they could find to dull the pain of a marriage that wasn't working. Today we deal with the issue more directly, and sometimes that involves ending the relationship.

When Gail and Fred got married, he didn't want to have children, but she was sure he'd change his mind once they had settled into their life together and he saw how important it was to her. To her surprise, Fred has only gotten more entrenched in his view over the eight years they've been married, pointing out continually how their friends' lives are limited by having young children. He loves to travel and sail, and doesn't want to give up the enormous amounts of time and money required to raise children. Gail is thirty-eight years old, and beginning to realize that she may have to choose between Fred and having children.

Unmet expectations often develop when people marry without being fully aware of their own needs, wants, and drives, but even veterans in their second or third marriages can have unmet expectations. Valerie and Jeff understood when they married that she was much more outgoing than he was. Her career was very important to her, and after work most nights she liked to spend time with friends and was very involved in local politics. Jeff preferred staying home, having a quiet dinner, and putting his feet up with a book or television.

They both expected that when they got married, their differences would work in their favor and support the relationship. He would give her an incentive to be less driven, to stay home and relax more; she would make it easier for him to spend time with other people and extend himself more. Unfortunately, it didn't work out that way. They found that they shared less and less of their lives, had very little to talk about, and eventually felt that the only thing they had in common was living in the same house.

Again, having differences is by no means a recipe for disaster. They can be worked out and this process can actually strengthen and enrich a relationship. But often when we feel that our needs aren't being met, or that our desires aren't being recognized and appreciated, we have a tendency to withdraw from the relationship, to stop loving or expressing our love as much. That makes the other person withdraw, and can eventually create hurts that are hard to mend.

3. What were your expectations going into the marriage?

We all grew up hearing about Cinderella and Prince Charming and may unconsciously hold these stories as life truths. Whether or not we are aware of it, some part of us may still believe that good, passive, beautiful girls get magical help to find eternal love with rich, handsome princes . . . or that brave, dashing boys who persevere always find gorgeous, angelic girls who become perfect, devoted wives.

Sometimes our expectations about marriage aren't much more realistic.

Many women think, "I'm going to open up this strong, silent husband of mine. With me, his feelings will come bubbling to the surface and he will be saved." This expectation is rarely realized. A common male fantasy is finding not only a replacement for mother, but someone who is also a fantastic lover. Other common expectations are:

- "He'll provide me with financial security forever; I'll never have to think about money again."
- "She will be the perfect wife who makes a beautiful home, anticipates my every need, and has a delicious dinner on the table each night. Our life at home will be perfectly harmonious, filled with lovely things and happy, beautiful children."
- "He will bring excitement and adventure to my life; I'll never be bored with him around."
- "Sex will be absolutely fantastic all the time."
- "Finally, someone who appreciates me enough to make my life easy and give me all the strokes I deserve."

Knowing what your expectations were gives you a deeper understanding of why the marriage didn't work, and where your resentments may lie.

4. How long did you want it to take to get the divorce?

If you wanted to get it over as quickly as possible and then found yourself in the midst of a long, drawn-out procedure, you probably felt frustrated and thwarted. Resentment or anger at the slowness of the other person, the lawyers, or the court may be part of your divorce hangover.

On the other hand, you may have wanted to drag the process out, hoping that you might get a more favorable settle-

32 DIVORCE HANGOVER

ment, make the other person suffer, or perhaps even get back together. If it went very quickly, you may still feel frustrated or upset. (If you hoped the divorce would be long and painful, you may want to examine your motives.)

If you are in the process of a divorce now, tell the truth about how long you want it to take. If you realize that you want to draw it out, ask yourself why. If you want to complete it as soon as you can, talk to all the parties concerned and if possible agree on some dates. Be prepared to make some adjustment if your pace is very different. You'll come out ahead in the long run.

5. What was your first priority in the divorce?

Your first priority may have been getting out of the marriage as quickly as possible, the well-being of the children, having the divorce be amicable, getting a good financial settlement, freedom, or whatever was important to you at that time.

Or, you may not have set any priorities at all and simply "winged it," handling issues as they arose.

If you knew what your first priority was and you stuck to it, you are less likely to have a divorce hangover. If you did not have a specific priority to guide your steps, or if it was thwarted, the results may have been brutal. You may have residual anger about things not working out the way you wanted them to, or not getting what you wanted out of the divorce.

My ex-husband and I decided that the children's well-being would be the priority in our divorce, and that decision got us through the rough times. Whenever we got bogged down, we went back to how the children's well-being would be affected.

If you are involved in a divorce now, I can't emphasize enough the value of setting your first priority for moving through this process. Your priority determines the answers to almost all the other questions that arise. It gives you a long-term goal and keeps you on track.

You will want other things from the divorce and it is important to rank these lesser priorities, but there will be one thing you want above all else and that thing must be your focus.

6. What was the greatest benefit to you?

You probably weren't thinking along these lines during the divorce itself, but by now you may have some perspective. You may be aware of some good things that have happened in your life as a result of the divorce, some benefits you've accrued by taking that step. Among the benefits that people often mention are:

- Increased sense of power and independence
- Freedom to explore other relationships
- Relationships with children that have become deeper through the adversity
- Career changes that were difficult at the time, but have turned out to be beneficial
- More flexibility to grow in individual ways
- Lost twenty pounds

No matter how difficult your divorce or severe your divorce hangover, it's likely that *something* positive came out of the experience.

SUMMARY

- To resolve the divorce hangover, you must examine and answer the 6 key questions as you would have during the divorce, and as you would now.

- The answers to these questions initiate your decision-making process, the key to resolving your divorce hangover.

◆

WORKBOOK EXERCISES

◆

1. Answer each cornerstone question according to your reality at the time of the divorce, and then according to your present reality.

2. Make note of your feelings regarding these questions (helplessness, confusion, anger, loss of control, etc.) These are the trigger points of your hangover.

STEP **3**   ◇   ◇   ◇   ◇   ◇   ◇

Count Your Losses

Divorce is devastating. That is a fact of life. It ranks as the #2 life crisis after the death of a spouse. Although divorced people experience enormous loss, they do not get the support that society extends to people whose spouses have died.

The divorce hangover begins in response to the staggering losses and changes of divorce, and the fear of even greater losses to come. It is important to understand exactly what you have lost. Remember, after divorce, loss and change occur for everyone—whether male or female and regardless of who initiated the breakup, or how amicable the proceedings may have seemed.

WHAT YOU LOSE

Divorce affects every area of your life: relationships, finances, physical surroundings, personal identity, home, health, family, and social situation. The losses strike at the very core of who you are, how you see yourself, and how others see you . . . and they seem to go on forever.

Everyone experiences his or her own specific, individual losses, but even this list of common ones is overwhelming:

- *Loss of the relationship.* No matter how bad it was, no matter who initiated the divorce, the loss is painful to both parties.
- *Loss of your expectations for the future.* You may have had a "happily ever after" dream—a beautiful home, perfect children, a devoted spouse. It doesn't matter if your fantasy was unrealistic; if you had the dream, it's easy to feel betrayed by fate, by your ex-spouse, and even by yourself.

  Perhaps your hopes for the marriage were more realistic: companionship, sex, financial security, someone to keep house for you, someone with whom to share holidays, camping trips, and even the late news. Even if your expectations were absolutely reasonable, it didn't work out that way and you have experienced a devastating loss.
- *Loss of financial structure and security.* For some people, this means reestablishing credit, or a change in lifestyle. But for others, the economic loss can be devastating and become a matter of sheer survival.
- *Loss of the children,* or at least daily contact with the children. You may not get to kiss them good-night every night. You may feel you have to work harder to make things perfect when you do see them. You miss out on the natural flow, the give and take that happens when families live together. Even if the children live with you, you must deal with loss when they go off for weekends, vacations, or holidays with the other parent.
- *Loss of self-esteem and self-confidence.* In our society, divorce is often mistakenly perceived as a failure, or even a sin. No one feels good about not making another person happy or not being able to make a relationship work. For many people, marriage is a way to define who they are

and to feel like able, upright, lovable people with a place in their community. Divorce takes away that structure. Very few people have a strong enough sense of their intrinsic self-worth to say, "I'm still okay, I'm still me."

- *Loss of sex with that person.* Sexuality is a large part of who we are. If sex was an important part of the marriage, or a part that escaped unscathed when the rest of the relationship fell apart, then this is a tremendous loss. If sex was only a habit, or part of a destructive power struggle, there was some payoff in that for you, and you've lost whatever the payoff was.

- *Loss of someone with whom to share familiar daily routines, burdens, and experiences.* After my divorce, I realized that it was always my turn to change light bulbs. Gardening had been my joy, but it became a chore when there was no one to help. There is no one with whom to share decisions, help with the kids if you are sick, or talk about the day. You lose your date for social events, someone with whom to go places, eat dinner, and share a bed.

- *Loss of friends.* Some people may have seen you as part of a couple and are not interested in you as a single friend. You may even seem threatening to married friends.

- *Loss of approval.* As many divorces as there are and as much as attitudes have changed, a social stigma still exists. It doesn't matter that in your efforts to grow, you simply discovered that you were in the wrong soil and were willing to go through the trauma of pulling yourself up and putting down roots in another, more nurturing place. Divorce is still against the social rules and, in a sense, you become an outlaw. It looks as if you can't stick to your commitments, as if you have been a bad spouse and maybe even a bad parent.

- *Loss of identity as part of a couple.* You are no longer Mr. and Mrs., Sally and Bill. You are just Sally, or just Bill. In places where the world moves two-by-two, this can be particularly painful.

- *Loss of the* habit *of the relationship.* You may no longer love the other person, but there is a gap, a loss of equilibrium when he or she is suddenly not there—even if most of your interaction was unpleasant.

- *Loss of order, permanence, and predictability*. Your world becomes ambiguous, unclear, uncertain, and you reflect these qualities. You don't think you can count on anything and feel out of control.

- *Loss of possessions*. Old photos, the rowing machine, the blender, the house, the end table, the dog. Often the monetary value has nothing to do with the depth of the loss.

- *Loss of "home."* Even if you get the house, it is not the same home without the other person. This can be an especially difficult loss for men, who are not as likely to be "nesters" and to create another "home" wherever they are.

- *Loss of power*. In some social environments, there is also a loss of power or status in not being part of a married couple. Invitations may not be extended because you are single or because your spouse is the preferred guest.

- *Loss of family*—not just loss of being a family yourselves, but loss of the in-laws. Many people have strong attachments to their partners' families. These relationships suffer in a divorce, and are sometimes destroyed entirely.

- *Loss of traditional holidays*. Whether or not you have the kids, and regardless of how you celebrate or don't celebrate holidays, you have lost the way it used to be.

EVERYTHING CHANGES

All of these losses have corresponding and equally devastating changes. The blank spot on a wall where a picture used to hang can be a daily, or hourly, reminder of the way things used to be. Changes in your schedule, a change in your name, changes in the way bills are paid—even these kinds of relatively minor alterations can be enormously upsetting. The larger changes can be devastating: a move to a new house or city, life without the children, massive financial upheaval, etc.

Not all the changes around divorce are negative, but all of them are hard.

Human beings have a natural resistance to change. We almost always prefer the familiar to the unfamiliar, even if the familiar isn't so great. A new job can be difficult and uncomfortable for the first few weeks, even if it is a big promotion. A new house can seem strange, even if we needed and wanted to make the change.

One of Dorothy's big complaints was that Hal never knew when he'd be home, leaving her on call to have dinner ready at unpredictable times. After the divorce, she could eat whenever she wanted, but found herself irritable as dinnertime approached. She realized that she was bored by the routine, that she missed the drama and adrenaline of the "hurry up and wait" dinners, even though, in fact, she preferred to eat at 7:00 every night.

It's natural to feel disoriented, out of control, helpless, angry, or guilty in the midst of change. This is a time of grasping at straws. Your instinct is to try and get everything back the way it was as quickly as possible. *When you can't do this, when the losses and changes won't go away, the frustration and pain are almost unbearable.* Your very survival seems threatened, and this calls up a natural, primitive instinct to protect yourself. It feels as if the world has been turned upside down, and it has.

TAKING STOCK

In order to face your losses, you have to know exactly what they are. I asked Stan in a counseling session to make a list of how his life had been before the divorce and how it was now, after the divorce. His BEFORE list included "house, yard, neighbors." His AFTER list read, "apartment in concrete complex, no yard, loss of financial equity and security."

Then I asked him to make lists of how he *felt* before and after the divorce. The BEFORE list was upbeat and optimistic:

"self-confident, secure, emotionally supported, good sense of humor, future bright, part of family and social group, intelligent, alert, strong." The AFTER list was a stark contrast: "scared, a failure, angry, hopeless, anxious, uncertain, bitter, alone, confused, unequipped to cope, helpless."

Stan had suffered change and loss in every aspect of his life, but he had not realized the extent of these losses or noticed how his image of himself had shifted.

Very few people have an accurate idea of what their losses and changes actually are until they sit down and start making lists.

SUMMARY

- Divorce hangover begins in response to the losses and changes caused by the divorce.

- It occurs regardless of gender, who initiated the divorce, or how amicable the proceedings may have been.

- Divorce hangover continues until you recognize and accept the losses and changes of the divorce.

◆

WORKBOOK EXERCISES

◆

1. Make a list in your workbook of all the losses discussed in this chapter.

2. Highlight the ones that have affected you most.

3. For each loss, describe what you felt.

4. List the changes caused by your divorce and your emotional response to each one.

5. What were you most afraid would happen as a result of the divorce?

6. Which of these fears were eliminated in the divorce settlement? Which are still present?

7. How would you describe yourself and your life before the divorce?

8. How would you describe yourself now?

STEP **4** ◇   ◇   ◇   ◇   ◇   ◇

Recognize Hangover Anger

Anger is the core emotion of divorce. The hangover begins when clean, honest anger at the losses and changes of divorce is converted into a secondary, once-removed anger—usually directed toward your ex-spouse, his or her new partner, their children, or even your new partner.

ANGER ONCE-REMOVED

The losses and changes are so painful that many people will do anything to avoid feeling them. When you don't face these losses directly, you don't experience the natural anger that they create.

Anger not faced doesn't go away; it is redirected. A divorce hangover begins when anger becomes directed toward whatever or whoever (including yourself) you consider responsible for the divorce. It becomes a protective device to keep you from feeling the pain of all that loss.

Grant had loved Jackie since high school and built his whole life around their relationship. When she told him after two years of marriage that she had fallen in love with Patrick and was leaving, Grant was devastated. He simply couldn't face the fact that his great love didn't love him anymore. He had lost the most important thing in his life, and on top of everything else he felt like a complete fool.

Instead of experiencing and expressing his anger at those losses, he redirected it toward Jackie's new lover. Patrick became the villain, and Grant could act out against him with threatening phone calls and even a fistfight, rather than deal directly with his feelings about all that he had lost.

CLEAN ANGER

Divorce is a kind of death; it is healthy and natural to mourn the end of a marriage and the loss of expectations, illusions, and false hopes—and an important part of that grieving process is *anger*.

In *On Death and Dying,* Elizabeth Kubler-Ross cites the five stages of grief as denial, anger, bargaining, depression, and acceptance. When you finally admit your loss and experience that pain, you are likely to be furious. If you let yourself experience the clean, raw, natural anger of grief, you can avoid a hangover.

You have a right to be angry, and to express your anger. It's not fair that your marriage is over. You did the best you could and it didn't work out. You may feel like railing against fate, "I set out to have a good marriage, I did everything I could, and I wanted it to work out!" This kind of anger resolves into acceptance, and has an end. At some point, it is over.

If you can't let yourself grieve the end of the marriage, then it's not really over for you. Some part of you can still pretend those losses never happened, or that you will wake up someday and everything will be back where it was. It's not that you *haven't* lost something; you just aren't telling yourself the truth about it. You are living in an illusion—frozen in time, stuck back in the marriage, and unable to move forward.

Sharon said, "As long as I didn't cry and scream about losing the house, I felt I hadn't really lost it somehow. Of course, I *had* lost it. We'd put it on the market, and other people had bought it and moved in. But part of me still lived there, even though it no longer had anything to do with my real life. I felt kind of funny and had to push myself a little to let go and bottom out, to scream and cry about losing that beautiful, beautiful home. But if I hadn't, I'd probably still be 'living' there."

TRICKY BUSINESS

Hangover anger is slippery. You can't control it, you can't release it appropriately, and sometimes you can't even *find* it until it suddenly erupts.

"I just couldn't get rid of the anger," Kevin said. "Whenever I thought about how she took me to the cleaners in the settlement, I sat down and fired off a scathing letter to her. I couldn't figure out what else to do, even though it usually made me feel even worse."

Since Kevin's anger was directed at his ex-wife rather than at its true source—the losses and changes that had turned his life upside down—it never was released. It was a loose cannon that never stopped firing, but never hit the target because it was pointing in the wrong direction.

A PERFECT TARGET

The most frequent target of once-removed, hangover anger is your ex-spouse, the person without whom there would *be* no loss or change, the person who seems to be standing between you and your ability to recapture the past. That person—or his or her new mate—becomes the villain, the one responsible for all the hurt and pain.

This is not a conscious decision. Usually you are not even aware of redirecting the anger, but it shows up in a variety of ways. Here are a few:

- *Revenge:* Carolyn had tried to ruin her ex-husband in the financial settlement, and their court battle became extremely ugly. "I'd lost my marriage and somebody was going to pay for it. I knew—somewhere *very* deep inside me—that he was hurt, angry, and bewildered, too. But I couldn't have cared less. I was fighting for my life, and I went after him with both barrels. I made that guy *pay* for what he'd done to me and the kids. Of course, he came back at me with *four* barrels and two lawyers.

   "Neither of us had a clue we were doing all this just to keep from feeling the pain. It was totally unconscious. Who knew? Instead of *avoiding* pain, we were really just creating *more* of it. It was crazy. . . ."

- *Blame:* Frank, who had left his alcoholic wife, said, "I kept thinking of her in that house and obsessing that if it weren't for her and her damned drinking, I could be living there, too, and we would be happy."

- *Sabotage:* Jerry paid all his bills on time except for one— his alimony check to Ellen. He knew that Ellen relied on his check to make the mortgage payment and that the bank charged her a late fee when it didn't arrive on time. Sometimes he "forgot" to sign the check so that by the time it was returned, signed, and sent back, another week and a half had passed. (He admitted that he smiled as he licked the envelope.)

He told me later, "I felt cornered, and so I attacked. Ellen was the easiest target."

- *Forced and Inappropriate Control:* Betty told me, "I just wanted to fight my way out of all the upheaval and disruption, to find some firm ground to stand on, to somehow say, 'This is who I am. This is where I am. This is what I'm going to do.' "

One way that Betty made her stand was by refusing to drop her three sons off at Ted's office on Friday nights. This meant that he had to drive an hour out to the house, and an hour and a half back to his apartment, after a twelve-hour work day (he worked overtime to provide more child support). Her lack of cooperation irritated him, started his weekend with the boys on a sour note, and aggravated Betty's boyfriend because their Friday nights out couldn't begin until 10:00. And when they finally did get together, she spent most of the evening complaining about Ted.

ANGER WITH A LIFE OF ITS OWN

Hangover anger takes on a life of its own. It doesn't even have to be triggered; it's just there—always and everywhere. It becomes your baseline point of view, the fundamental attitude from which you relate to other people and the world.

David's anger had taken on such a life of its own that his ex-wife, Sandy, didn't have to do much to make him furious. He lived in a perpetual state of turmoil. In his mind, she was the source of all his pain, the arch-villain who was out to make him miserable.

When she actually did do something like take him back to court, he went to town, retaliating by telling their friends ugly stories about her and being late with alimony and child support.

Hangover anger so sapped his energy that even his career was suffering. In our initial counseling session, he said, "My whole life is in shambles. Now even my career is up for grabs." Throughout the discussion, he kept talking about "that damned woman and that damned divorce."

David saw that he had not wanted to face the loss of his children and home, and so he had misdirected that anger toward Sandy and life in general. He was no longer angry *at* people or things; he was simply *angry*.

THE ULTIMATE RELEASE

How can you tell if yours is the clean, natural, healthy anger of grief or the self-destructive anger of the divorce hangover? The clean anger of grief cleanses your spirit and goes away. Divorce hangover anger persists and turns ugly, attacking both the people you hold responsible for your bad feelings and innocent bystanders. If you are ever in doubt, ask yourself how far removed the anger is from its true source—the losses and changes. The farther removed it is, the less healthy it is.

Peg was chronically furious at her husband because he was not giving her enough money. She realized her anger was the result of being broke after the divorce and not yet being able to find good work. The anger at her husband was futile (he was a disabled veteran) and kept her in her divorce hangover. *When you recognize how you have misdirected anger over loss and change into anger against your ex-spouse or others, a huge portion of that anger simply disappears.*

The anger that remains is much easier to manage because you understand it. You know how it works, what it is trying to do, and where it is likely to show up. You are always a step ahead of it.

There is no magic formula to letting go of anger. It is very simple. You have to *want* to give it up—notice when it raises its head, and let it go consciously. You have to choose being happy over being right. The clearer you become about where your hangover anger lies, how it works, what it is protecting, and what it is costing you, the more quickly and easily it dissolves.

These exercises will take you through the process of releasing hangover anger.

SUMMARY

- Anger can be a protective device to avoid the pain of the losses and changes of divorce.

- Divorce hangover anger usually targets the ex-spouse and the divorce.

- It takes many forms, but always holds you in the past as a victim of circumstances instead of a person in charge of his or her own destiny.

◆

WORKBOOK EXERCISES

◆

1. What forms does your anger take?

2. Next to each behavior, write who the target is.

3. What reactions does your anger prompt from these target people?

4. If there is a reaction from them, what do you do next?

5. What do they do in response to that?

6. Does your anger produce any change?

7. Recognizing that loss and change are the causes of your anger, rank the ones that anger you most.

8. Think of ways, post-divorce, that you can bring some of these things back into your life without harming anyone.

STEP **5** ◇   ◇   ◇   ◇   ◇   ◇

Unmask Your Hangover

Hangover anger has many clever disguises. If you recognize it, it will start to weaken and disappear. It has to stay hidden in order to survive.

THE COVER-UP

Any good disguise presents illusion as reality, so it really does feel as if you are angry at the other person and that your anger is justified.

Karen and Charles were divorced five years ago, but she keeps dragging him back into court to revise the financial settlement. Charles says, "I don't understand it. No matter how much I give her, it isn't enough."

When they were divorced, Karen simply couldn't deal with the loss of their beautiful home, her standing in the community, and the connection with his family, with whom she was very close. Taking Charles back to court again and again gave her an outlet for the anger and also maintained her connection with him, with their marriage, and with his family.

That's not how it felt to Karen, though. In her mind, she was doing it so that justice would be done and she would get what she deserved. He had promised her a certain lifestyle and then broken that promise. To her, the anger had nothing to do with loss; it was a question of right and wrong.

Perhaps Karen *was* right and had a perfectly good claim on everything she was demanding, but she was ignoring her own responsibility in the marriage and her participation in the divorce, and keeping herself in the role of a victim. She was also ignoring the present reality, which was that she was no longer married to Charles. As long as she overlooked those two things, the hangover would continue.

Your anger and outrage may seem as real and justifiable as

Karen's righteous indignation at Charles. The giveaway is how you feel. Are you happy? Are you relaxed? Are you spending energy on the old relationship, or are you getting on with your life? Are you accepting your own responsibility in all this? Are you accepting life as it is, or pretending it is how you would like it to be?

MASKS

Everyone masks the hangover differently, but because they are unconscious, these masks are often hard to pinpoint.

If you have a divorce hangover, you have a mask. Without the mask, you would have to face the pain, the anger at your losses, and your responsibility for your life as it is now. If you did that, you would not have a hangover.

These are a few of the many masks a hangover can wear:

- *The Sexual Mask:* Bill couldn't say enough bad things about Cheryl to their friends, but was aggressively sexual when they did "run into each other." This set up a "star-crossed lovers" drama between the two of them which they both enjoyed playing out to the audience of their friends. "What a great couple they made! What passion! What a tragedy it didn't work out!" This drama kept them from having to admit that their marriage was over or feeling the pain of that loss. It also kept them both out of other relationships.

- *The "Poor Me" Mask:* Lisa has been depressed ever since her divorce from Saul two years ago, but whenever he is around the depression becomes much worse.

  When he comes to see the kids, she greets him at the door with a martyred look, a sigh, and perhaps a "reluctant" tear in her eye. She doesn't know how she is going to make ends meet this month with only that small amount of child support, and Tommy's extra soccer expenses made the burden worse. She's afraid Samantha's "I hate boys" stage has something to do with what her father did to her. She supposes it doesn't matter that she's too old for another relationship or that men no longer find her attractive; she's just trying to make ends meet and hold herself together for the sake of the children so that they, too, won't be ruined by the divorce.

This mask hides a very angry woman, but Lisa won't have a chance to deal with that anger as long as the "poor me" mask is in place.

- *The Crazed Bitch/Bastard Mask:* Boyd and Dayna have been the original Bickersons since their divorce and just missed being cast in Hollywood's divorce hangover epic, *The War of the Roses.*

  She tries to bleed him with a new financial settlement almost every year. When this happens, he delights in revealing the details of her other relationships, even when the children are present. Last Thanksgiving, he sent her a dozen dead roses. When he came to pick up the children later that afternoon, she threw cold leftover gravy on him.

  Recently they found themselves at the same cocktail party. Loud, ugly words were exchanged and before the evening was over, she had drawn blood with a fingernail slash to Boyd's new wife's cheek.

  These are very powerful emotions, but it's not as simple as it seems. If Boyd and Dayna's problems were strictly with one another, the anger would release after it was expressed. The strength of their hangovers suggests how deep their losses were.

There are as many masks as there are people with divorce hangovers, and you know best what yours looks like. When you can get beyond the mask to what you are really feeling, you begin dealing with reality rather than illusion.

THE FACES OF ANGER

Anger shows up differently in assertive and nonassertive people, and can turn either outward toward others or inward toward oneself.

Assertive people tend to act out. They move, but they move

in circles. They call in the middle of the night, never miss a chance to be sarcastic or critical, spend hours figuring out how to thwart the other person, and may use the children or money as tools to "get" their ex-spouse. They send their kids to the other parent's house with messages like: "Dad, Coach says I have to have a helmet to play hockey and Mom says she can't buy it." They may also instruct their children to say hurtful things to the other parent's new mate.

The ultimate divorce hangover for this personality takes the form of actually killing the ex-spouse. All too often we read of the tragic murders of ex-spouses and even children and other relatives by a crazed and enraged ex-spouse.

Less assertive people are likely to be depressed, which is anger turned inward, the "flight" part of our instinctive "flight or fight" reaction to fear and pain. Rather than acting out, they tend to withdraw and run away. This is fine for a while if you just need time alone to heal, but can become destructive if you hide because you never want to risk being hurt again.

Depression is anger bottled up inside. Life seems filtered through a screen, without spontaneity or expression. But even depression can be used to punish the other person if he or she can't get you to talk, smile, or communicate.

Sometimes depression becomes mired in self-pity. It can be an attempt to garner sympathy and make others feel responsible for your situation, but unfortunately, it usually backfires and pushes others away.

Depression brings on inertia. Everything stagnates and deteriorates. You don't take care of the house, the kids, or yourself. Pete tried to save his marriage by working through his "emotional kinks" in therapy. Just as he felt he was making real progress, his wife, Helen, "bailed out." He was desperate to make the marriage work and pleaded with her to hang in there just a little longer, but she insisted on leaving and they agreed to be friends. There were no children and they had enough money for each of them to buy and furnish separate homes.

Helen went on with her life, devoting more time to her career and eventually becoming interested in another man. Pete knew that there was a new life out there for him somewhere, but was too afraid to explore it. He began to feel sorry for himself and lose himself in the inertia of depression.

He was angry that he had treated Helen badly during their marriage, and even angrier that he hadn't been given another chance to show her the man he felt he had become, but he was afraid to say much to her for fear of driving her even farther away. Instead, he turned it all back in on himself. He wasn't working, he slept a lot, the new house went to ruin, and he was preoccupied with the second chance he never got.

The ultimate divorce hangover for this more passive personality is suicide. Rosemary became more and more withdrawn in the year following her divorce until, finally, she rarely left the house. She made it clear that she wanted to be left alone, and so that's what people did. Everyone was so surprised when she showed up at a cocktail party one June night that no one really noticed she was dressed entirely in beige. She had always worn bold colors. She was gracious to everyone and, although she left a bit early, her friends were glad to see that she was making an effort to get out.

A week later, she was found dead from an overdose of pills. All her affairs were in order and she had even left notes covering every detail of the children's schedule, down to when their clothes had to be picked up at the cleaners. Her friends realized that the night of the cocktail party, she had come to say good-bye.

SUMMARY

- The divorce hangover is a mask that covers the real, unresolved pain of the divorce.

- Discovering what your mask looks like helps you manage the hangover and take responsibility for your actions.

♦

WORKBOOK EXERCISES

♦

1. Which mask(s) do you wear to act out your hangover anger? The sexual mask? The "poor me" mask? The crazed bitch/bastard mask?

2. Is your anger more assertive (directed outward) or non-assertive (directed inward)? Give examples.

3. Do you see a relationship between your hangover mask and the form your anger takes? What is that connection?

STEP **6** ◇   ◇   ◇   ◇   ◇   ◇

Let the Victim Go

It's easy to feel victimized in a divorce—even if you are the one leaving, but especially if you are the one who is "left."

I have heard people say things like:

- "He's made my life miserable."
- "If it hadn't been for the hell she put me through, I would have gotten that promotion."
- "She's turning my children against me."
- "He took my best years . . . who's going to want me now?"
- "I feel so cheated!"

All of these people felt like victims. Many of them may actually *be* victims, but continuing to hold themselves that way will not get them what they want or help them release the hangover. *You may have been victimized, but you don't have to remain a victim.* The other person may have hurt you, but you are not powerless. At the very least, you have power over your attitudes.

FEELING VICTIMIZED

Janet put Ron through dental school. Eight years later, he left her for his office manager. They have no children, but Janet hasn't worked in six years. She got their house in the settlement, but she will have to reduce her standard of living substantially unless she gets more alimony than seems likely. Worse, being left for a younger woman made her feel old and unattractive.

"It's my worst nightmare," she said. "Every time I try to sit down and figure things out, I just wind up crying and wondering how he could do this to me. Then I turn on TV and cry myself to sleep. The next morning, I start in again but the same thing happens. I just can't shake myself out of this."

Janet's situation is difficult, but at some point, she has to say to herself, "Okay, this is the hand I've been dealt. I can either go back to bed and cry for the rest of my life, or I can play this hand. It doesn't make what he did right, but for my own sake, I have to let go of this. What can I do to start feeling better? What can I do to change the situation so that it's better for me?"

She has to stop figuring out who was right or wrong, reach out, and pick up the reins of her own life. If she doesn't pick up those reins, nothing is ever going to change. It doesn't matter who was right or wrong; all that matters is her happiness and her future.

Janet also has to accept her share of responsibility for what happened in the marriage and the divorce, and understand that all she has to work with now is her present reality. She has to go on from here and begin designing the rest of her life.

BEING VICTIMIZED

What if the situation is so extreme that it really seems as if you *are* a victim? Suppose:

- Your husband called you from work one afternoon and announced that, after twenty years of marriage and four children, he was leaving you for his twenty-year-old secretary. You were content in the marriage, or thought you were. You thought *he* was content! You'd done nothing to deserve this. You didn't see it coming and didn't want it to happen.

- You came home one night and found a note on the kitchen table from your wife saying that she had cleaned out the bank account and was starting a new life where you would never find her. You thought that you were best friends as well as marriage partners, that you told each other everything. This feels like the ultimate betrayal. Somewhere along the line, you lost touch with what was really going on.

Rejection is immensely painful, particularly when you have trusted the other person. Sometimes there is no way to avoid feeling like a victim—at first.

The problem is that continuing to see yourself as a victim freezes the situation in place. If you cast yourself in the role of someone who can't do anything about it, then nothing is going to *get* done. The other person certainly isn't going to come to your rescue, as much as you might wish he or she would.

In order to get out of the situation and move forward, you have to assume the point of view—rightly or wrongly—that you are *not* a victim, that you have dominion over your own life and can affect what happens. You have to adopt the viewpoint that, at the very least, you can change your attitude from negative to positive.

You can have some good cries and throw as many fits as you like, *but then sit down and take stock of where you are now.*

MYTHS OF FAILURE, BLAME, AND GUILT

These myths have a lot to do with people feeling victimized in divorce. They are lies you can no longer afford.

Failure. Divorce is not a personal failure, even though it may seem that way at times. The *relationship* may have failed, but *you* didn't fail.

Sometimes it's hard to think about that other person without also thinking of his or her failings:

- He called you fat, then tempted you with a fancy dinner out just when you'd started a diet.
- She was rotten to your children—cold, petty, and unresponsive.
- He refused sex and made you feel undesirable. It was part of a power game that never let up.
- She was dominating, controlling, and insensitive. You couldn't even change the TV channel without abuse.
- He cheated on you, and then violated your agreement to confess if either of you went outside the marriage for sex.

There is no denying all the terrible things that happened. The facts are not arguable; those people did do those awful things, and it *hurt*.

You can't go back and change what happened, but you can change how you choose to deal with those facts. You can hold them to you, playing them over and over in your mind, counting all the ways your ex-spouse failed you and caused you to be a failure in the marriage—or you can just let them go.

Letting go doesn't mean that what the other person did was right, or that some of your own mistakes were right. It just means there's no sense in holding on because it will only keep you stuck. Do this for yourself, not for the other person.

If you think of your ex-spouse as a failure, you'll think of yourself as a failure, too. If you go looking for failings, you'll probably find them on both sides. The more Faith thought about Chuck's infidelity, his smoking, and his habit of not picking up his clothes, the harder it was to avoid thoughts about her own affair and the three cocktails she had every night. She even started to feel guilty for never cooking him a meal, something he often threw in her face during the marriage.

Feelings of failure produce no positive results and can keep you from getting involved in new relationships. For your own sake, get rid of them quickly.

Blame. Blame and guilt are flip sides of the same coin, and both are a waste of time and energy.

Again, it may seem that the other person is to blame. When Glen and Sandra's marriage ended, there was no doubt in her mind that he was at fault. He ridiculed her in public and called her a "cow" in front of their friends, even though she was only slightly overweight. Then when they got home, he always wanted to have sex. The more abusive he had been, the more important this was to him and the less interested she was. Glen always won this power game by reminding her that he earned ten times what she did and was also supporting her daughter from a previous marriage.

In the year before they separated, Sandra had begun to suspect that this same dynamic was going on between Glen and her daughter, Sharie. Glen was also involved with speed and cocaine. He had never been physically violent with Sandra or Sharie, but he had threatened them and had trashed the house on more than one occasion.

It would be hard to find anyone to take Glen's part in this saga, but finally Sandra had to stop acting as judge and jury and step into the more important role of *taking care of herself.* Blaming Glen was justified, but it was getting her nowhere. For the sake of her own and her child's happiness and future, she had to let it go. Holding on to who's at fault has no part in a healthy person's life.

In counseling, Sandra also looked at her own part in this story. Why had she stayed, particularly when she thought Glen might be involving Sharie? What attitudes about herself had allowed her to put up with that level of abuse? These were necessary questions for her to ask, as long as she avoided the trap of feeling guilty or finding fault with herself for the past.

Guilt. Divorce and the less-than-saintly divorce hangover antics we engage in often create guilt, which is always lurking around the edges of our psyche waiting to pounce whenever we are vulnerable.

Diedre felt as though she had a double dose of divorce guilt because her religion forbade divorce. "It seemed to take over my whole mind and absorb all my thoughts," she said. "There was no room for anything else. I let Terry get away with murder because I felt so guilty, and that made me even more angry at him. I had to take myself by the hand and *make* myself give it up. It was an act of will, nothing less!"

This is often what it takes to get rid of guilt—an act of will. You need to examine why you feel guilty and whether you can do anything about the situation that prompts it. If there is nothing you can do then the only alternative is to let go of the guilt. Different methods work for different people: books, talking with friends, therapy, support groups. You have to find your own most effective way to deal with it, *but you must release the guilt*. This is not an optional assignment. Guilt is pure poison.

THE BOOTSTRAP APPROACH

There is a fine line between standing up for yourself and blaming the other person, between examining your own issues and falling prey to guilt. If your ex-spouse did terrrible things, they are not figments of your imagination. Those deeds are real, and so is your pain. But in the end, that person's actions aren't as important as the attitude you take toward them.

It is impossible to let go of a divorce hangover when you feel like a victim.

To turn things around and shift your point of view from victim to victor, you'll have to pick yourself up by your own bootstraps. That means letting go of failure, blame, and guilt and adopting attitudes that move you forward.

A note of caution: There will always be irrational people who are driven to make others miserable. If someone is doing you physical or psychological harm, or threatening physical harm, use whatever legal, social, and law enforcement institutions are necessary to protect yourself, and stay as far away from that person as possible.

SUMMARY

- Failure, blame, and guilt distract you from your real purpose: accepting where you are and building a new, fulfilling life.

- Regardless of what your ex-spouse or others did to you, you can step out of the role of victim by adopting the point of view that you do have control over your life.

- Only by adopting this attitude and moving from victim to victor can you release the hangover.

WORKBOOK EXERCISES

1. Do you have feelings of failure, blame, or guilt about the divorce? Describe them.

2. Look at your divorce settlement and your ex-spouse's behavior. How do they make you feel like a victim?

3. Pick two specific situations in which you feel or felt victimized. Rewrite the script so that the outcome is victimless.

STEP **7** ◇   ◇   ◇   ◇   ◇   ◇

Cross the Abyss

The crucial moment in any divorce or in resolving your hangover comes when you finally realize that the life you led and the person you were *no longer exist*. That is a moment of terrible anguish—but it is also the beginning of your new life, a life free of the old pains and losses, a life you design to express the person you have become.

THE ABYSS

The abyss is that dark, unknown place between the past and the future, between where you've been and where you are going. It is like a deep chasm between two cliffs. To avoid or resolve the divorce hangover, you have to let go of the past completely, leap the abyss, and hang suspended there *even before you know what the future will look like*.

You leap the abyss when you realize that all the expectations you had about your marriage—companionship, physical intimacy, a shared life, financial security, love everlasting, whatever you thought you would have—are really gone.

This is an act of great courage. You are no longer who you were, and not yet who you will be. You don't have your old life, and you don't yet have your new life. The marriage is over, and there is nothing to replace it.

Why would you do this? Because until you cross the abyss and let go of the past completely, you can't find your vision or the design of your future. It doesn't work to try straddling the abyss with one foot in the past and the other feeling around out there for what the future will be like. You have to accept that your old life is over forever and that you'll never get it back.

Russ told me, "I didn't even know I was holding on to those last threads—the last details of the financial settlement—thinking that Allie and I might get back together because there was still a lot of sexual energy and flirting when we saw each other. Giving up on that idea was the hardest thing I ever did. I felt like there would be nothing left if I lost that last hope and admitted that Allie really wasn't coming back, that I would never live with my children again, or live in that house again."

WHAT KEEPS YOU STUCK

Fear of the abyss, of the sensation of being neither here nor there, is what keeps most people stuck in bad marriages, and in divorce hangovers.

Pam had been talking about leaving Randy for three years. He drank heavily, threatened to beat her up, had "accidentally" given their seven-year-old son a black eye, and was unfaithful.

The marriage had gone beyond difficult to destructive. Pam was constantly telling her friends and the people at work how awful Randy was and how she was going to leave him—but somehow, she never did. She planned to go after the holidays, then after their son had left for camp, then after she finished a big project at work, then when their lease was up. But all these milestones came and went, and Pam was still with Randy.

Finally the situation got so bad that she sought counseling. She realized she was afraid that no matter how bad it was with Randy, it would be worse if she didn't have *anyone!* She had to explore that fear thoroughly, but even so when Pam finally did leave, she did it on blind faith. That's how she *had* to do it. There was no way to prove beforehand that it would work out. She had to choose which was more important: her son and herself, or the chance that it would get better with Randy.

LETTING GO

When you leap into the abyss, you must let go of illusions and false hopes.

You must let go of:

- *The illusion* that you didn't *really* lose that person, that house, those children, or all the other parts of the life you shared. You may still go to the Saturday-night barbecue or the dance at the club, you may live in the same house and have all the same clothes in your closet, *but you are not the same person you were when you were married.*

Iris said, "It took me a while to stop clutching at this fantasy that things were pretty much the same in my life except that Sandy was making me miserable. He was still in my life. So what if I was just dealing with what a jerk he was? So what if all the connections were negative and awful? They were still *there*."

- *The false hope* that one day, somehow, you will get it all back. This ugly stuff will simply evaporate and, magically, perfection will return.

These illusions and false hopes are largely unconscious, which makes them even more dangerous. Very few of us would admit to having them; very few of us even know that we *do* have them. But if you are involved in a divorce hangover, they are probably hidden away in some corner of your mind.

DANGEROUS BRIDGES

Some people try to use a third person as a bridge over the abyss, hoping that a new relationship will ease the pain of losing the old one. This is dangerous. The new person may dull the pain for a time, but ultimately you have to experience the abyss alone. For you, the abyss may take an instant or several years— but it is not a place where you can be with another person.

If you truly honor the new relationship and want it to last, take care of the past before you try moving into the future. If you don't, you will just bring your past with you.

Others bury themselves in work in an effort not to feel the pain. You may need some diversion from the chaos, but not if it keeps you from facing facts. Workaholism can be just as much an escape as alcohol, overeating, or a new relationship.

The most dangerous bridge of all is the hangover, which keeps you connected to the past even though that old way of life no longer even exists. You need to say to yourself, "The life I lived with my ex-spouse is over and gone. I am in an entirely new and different place now. Even though this new place isn't familiar or comfortable, I have to let go of what was because it doesn't exist anymore. This new place is my only reality."

The sooner you cross the abyss, the sooner the healing process begins.

SUMMARY

- The abyss is the unavoidable gap between where you are now and where you want to be. It must be crossed whenever you make a change.

- The abyss is your bridge to the future.

WORKBOOK EXERCISES

1. Describe what the abyss means to you.

2. What false hopes do you still cling to about the past relationship?

3. Think of changes you have experienced in your life: new schools, adolescence to adulthood, moving to a new town, taking a new job. Describe how these changes felt: how you wished you could be in the old as well as in the new place, how sometimes you didn't want to make the change at all, how strange it felt thinking about the old situation once you were settled into the new one.

STEP **8**   ◊   ◊   ◊   ◊   ◊   ◊

Make Decisions

You can de-mystify divorce, and the divorce hangover, by thinking of them as a series of decisions to be made. Making decisions puts you on solid ground where you have control and moves you from the *emotional* into the *rational*.

POWER THROUGH DECISIONS

Paula got divorced when her sons were fourteen and sixteen. She kept the house but Greg was always either late with alimony and child support or he didn't pay them at all. She worked as a teacher's aide and her salary wasn't enough to pay the mortgage, feed two large and growing boys, keep them in basketball and baseball gear, and maintain the household. Paula's parents helped when they could, but their income was also limited and they had never entirely approved of Greg anyway, so Paula felt uncomfortable about accepting their support.

The drama and anxiety each month over which bills could be paid and which could not was making her crazy and she often took it out on the boys. Greg didn't have a lot of money, but what he did have, he spent on his convertible, his young girlfriend, and outings with the boys to Knicks and Mets games. All of this impressed the boys, and Greg made a point of telling them how much he loved them and wished Paula hadn't driven him away.

They began to hold her responsible for all the upheaval in their lives and she felt like she was losing them, especially as they started spending more time away from home for sports, dating, and trips with Greg. Her bitterness about the divorce, her financial bind, Greg's girlfriend, and the way he seemed to be poisoning the boys against her became almost paralyzing.

Paula needed to formulate her turmoil into specific questions that would form the basis for some major life decisions. Among the questions she asked herself were:

- What do I want to do about the nonpayment of alimony and child support? Is it worth dragging Greg back to court?
- Do I need to make more money? If so, how much and how can I do it?
- Do the boys need to get jobs after school and contribute to the household?
- Do I want the boys to continue going on these outings with Greg? Is it all right if his girlfriend goes along?
- What can I do about Greg's criticism, and the effect it has on the boys? Is there a way to talk to Greg, or to the boys, so that he will stop or so that it won't do as much damage?
- What can I do to get my relationship with the boys back on track?

Just coming up with these questions took courage, and Paula felt better about herself as soon as she sat down with her workbook and started tackling them one by one. The process went on for several days, but her investment of time and energy was well worth the effort.

She decided, among other things, to hire a lawyer and make sure Greg came through with the agreed-upon alimony and child support. She also limited the trips to one a month and stipulated that his girlfriend could not go with them. She decided to finish the one semester she needed to complete her B.A. so that she could get a better job, and swallowed her pride by asking her parents for a loan. They gave it to her gladly, and she set a cut-off date for this support. She also began seeing a counselor about her relationships with Greg and the boys.

Since the boys got after-school jobs to help with household expenses, they cast a much more objective eye on Greg, the convertible, and the girlfriend. They also feel like part of the team each time they contribute part of their earnings. They are beginning to have more respect for Paula and all that she has been doing.

The decisions Paula made don't matter as much as *the fact that she made them*. Sitting down and deciding what she was going to do turned her from a victim into a woman in charge of her own destiny. Things may get rough from time to time, but she is calling the shots now.

Whenever you feel agitated or angry, use this question and answer process to take charge. If contact with your ex-spouse is the issue, for example, you might want to ask yourself these kinds of questions:

- Do I want to have contact with him or her at all?
- If not, what do I have to do to take charge and make sure it doesn't happen?
- If I want to have the contact so I learn not to let it get to me, in what specific circumstances do I want to see him or her?
- What do I have to do to make sure I control those circumstances?
- What is the truth about what I feel when I see the other person?
- How would I like to be and feel when I see him or her?
- What can I do to move myself from where I am now into that place?

HOW IT WORKS

Making rational, conscious decisions empowers you in four ways:

1. *You put a stop to emotional confusion and take control.* Bobbie found herself sobbing uncontrollably in the week her divorce became final. She needed to shed those tears, but she also needed to go to work, get the kids to school, and get on with her life. She pulled herself together by asking these questions:

- How much money do we need each week to live?
- How much money do we have?
- Can I afford to keep the job I have now or do I need to get one that pays more?
- What can I do to start feeling better and take care of myself?
- Who would be a good support team for me right now?
- Do I really feel like taking that gang of kids to the movie on Saturday or can I get one of the other mothers to do it?

Once Bobbie got involved in answering these questions, she began to feel better. Making decisions helps you get your feet back on the ground. If nothing else, decide: "What is upsetting me? What can I do about it?"

2. *You bring your situation into clear focus and then start directing it.* You tell the truth about the present, and then create the future. As you make this process part of your daily life, clarity and confidence become habits. The more you practice, the more skilled you become.

3. *You discover what you want and where you want to go.* Each decision you make does two things: 1) It gives you a better grip on the situation, and 2) It moves you down the road toward ending your divorce hangover. You are no longer drifting aimlessly; you have a goal and are pursuing it.

Forrest hated the small apartment where he had been living since the divorce, and this made him think about how he'd never liked living in Indianapolis either. They had only moved there to be near Justine's family. One of the first decisions he made was to move back to Raleigh. That became the basis for many of his other decisions about finances, children, and career.

4. *You stay on top of the overwhelming number of decisions to be made.* During a divorce or in healing a divorce hangover (or even in living life!), the questions

keep piling up whether or not you are coming up with the answers. When decision-making becomes a natural, daily process, the questions don't get a chance to accumulate.

THE HABIT OF DECISION-MAKING

Decision-making makes you feel better about yourself and soon becomes a habit. I'm not suggesting that you should stuff all your emotions or become an unfeeling zombie. What I'm talking about is putting an end to the paralyzing, debilitating cycle of negative emotions associated with the divorce hangover.

Allow yourself an honest emotional response, but then decide what needs doing and do it. At least for now, it's important to choose head over heart. We have a right to our feelings, but we aren't children. If your breakfast doesn't magically appear on the table in the morning, you don't scream and cry and throw yourself on the floor; you cook it or go to a restaurant.

Brian found himself so paralyzed after the divorce that he couldn't even go to work. He stayed home in bed and watched television. After four days, he decided it was time to rejoin the living. He sat down and let one question lead to another until he had lifted himself out of the quagmire:

- When do I want to go back to work?
- What do I want my attitude to be when I do?
- What else do I need to do to normalize my life? Grocery shopping? Dry cleaning? Clean the house?
- How can I be good to myself during this transition period? Play more tennis? A weekend in the country? Buy some new clothes?

Making decisions is your lifeline. It's not something that is merely helpful, or a good idea; it is absolutely essential, the one thing guaranteed to keep your head above water during this process. It gives you an action plan for taking charge of your life.

◆

SUMMARY

The rewards of taking control and making decisions about the direction of your life are:
• You take the initiative and eliminate confusion.
• You face the situation as it is and do something about it.

◆

◆

WORKBOOK EXERCISES

◆

1. Think of a situation that obstructs your life.

2. Make a list of questions regarding the situation.

3. Outline a step-by-step plan to take you from being stuck to solving the problem and moving ahead.

STEP **9** ◇   ◇   ◇   ◇   ◇   ◇

Turn Negative Attitudes into Positive Ones

One of the most powerful skills you can master is the ability to turn negative thinking and situations into positive ones.

MANAGING YOUR ATTITUDES

Positive attitudes create positive behavior; negative attitudes create negative and self-destructive behavior. It's just that simple. The ending of a marriage is not a time to "go with the flow" and let yourself drift without a sail or rudder. You need to take charge.

After my husband and I separated, I woke up each morning thinking, "What am I doing?" When I let myself dwell on that, I realized that I really didn't have the slightest idea what I was doing. I learned that if I allowed these attitudes free rein, my thoughts deteriorated at an alarming rate. I had no choice but to push those thoughts away and *fill the vacuum quickly,* or I would be sucked down and lost.

What worked for me was filling the "vacuum" with specific things to do (chores, errands, exercises) and affirmative thoughts about how far I had come. I reminded myself of my long-term goals and plotted small steps that would lead to them. I immediately felt better about myself, the world, and my chances of surviving. With practice, I was able to keep the demons at bay and finally discovered that they had disappeared altogether.

Another thing that helped me get a grip and keep a positive focus was the phrase that became my battle cry: "Remember number one." When my thoughts started to whirl out of control, I just kept repeating that to myself until I calmed down and could start doing something positive. If you think a phrase like this would help you, come up with one that grounds you, keeps you focused in the present, and feeds you strength and energy. Some examples might be: "Remember the kids." "One step at a time." "I'm stronger today than I was yesterday." "Tomorrow is whatever I want to make it." "Today is mine to decide."

Managing attitudes also means managing your energy. You've taken on a life crisis, whether it is getting the divorce or healing the divorce hangover, and you probably have more adrenaline flowing through your system than usual. If you don't use that energy, it may start using you—so harness it and manage it in positive ways, depending on your needs. A good workout, or a strenuous walk with the kids, alone, or with a friend are all ways of releasing pent-up energy.

The key to managing your attitudes is to *see this as a chance for growth, insight, freedom, power, and a fresh start in life.* Opportunities like that don't come along every day.

ALCHEMY: NEGATIVE TO POSITIVE

Attitudes can become habitual. You may have attitudes that you developed after your divorce that no longer work for you, but that you forgot to discard. By not working, I mean they undermine your relationship with yourself and everyone else in your life. They no longer fit where you are now.

Now is the time to weed them out or transform them into positive points of view. These are some common negative attitudes that hangover sufferers need to change:

- *Fault-finding.* "I'm the good guy and the victim in this play; she (he) ruined my life."
- *Win/Lose.* "If he (she) wins, I lose. I have to grab at everything I can get."
- *Negative generalizations.* "Men (women) are out to get you." "Marriage is a rotten institution."
- *Self-pity.* "Nothing will ever be the same."
- *Escape.* "I'll just hide, and then no one will ever hurt me again."

Not only do these attitudes cast you in the role of victim, but they all suggest that you play it safe, don't stick your neck out, and protect yourself—except to pop up occasionally and blast the other guy, before hurrying back into the bunker.

These attitudes keep you stuck. The antidote is to become aware of exactly what your negative attitudes are, and take positive steps to turn them around.

SELF-SABOTAGE

Self-sabotage is a mass of negative attitudes that are raging out of control. Wherever you find the divorce hangover, you will find self-sabotage.

After her divorce, Barbara was trying to launch a design business but was sabotaging herself by not meeting deadlines and always running late for appointments. No matter how much time she allowed for preparation, she always felt behind, frazzled, and worn out during important presentations.

Her self-esteem was at a low ebb when she came to me, saying, "It amazes me that anyone would even want me to tell them how to arrange their living room furniture, let alone trust anything I have to say about colors or textures . . ."

As we talked, she kept mentioning that she was divorced. Actually, she didn't "just mention" it, but went into great detail about her ex-husband and how unfair she thought everything had been during the divorce. She spent more time discussing the bitterness she felt toward him than she did talking about her design business.

She had to manage two attitudes into a more positive vein: 1) her low self-esteem, and 2) her embittered, victimized stance toward her ex-husband.

Self-sabotage also occurs in personal areas, including:

- Not getting involved in new relationships because you are so depressed, angry, or unresolved about the past one.
- Damaging your relationship with your children by using them as pawns.
- Making things as difficult as possible for your ex-spouse, regardless of the high emotional cost to you.

NEW LANGUAGE FOR DIVORCE

Words have tremendous power to shape reality, and the words we use around divorce tend to be negative. We speak of the "trauma" of divorce and the "poor children," to say nothing of the words we use to describe ex-spouses! Consciously changing these negative words and associations to positive ones is a good way to transform your attitudes.

Divorce doesn't have to be a "crippling trauma" or a "devastation." It can be a "challenge," an "opportunity," a "transition," a "new beginning," a "life crisis prodding me from one way of living into a new, richer, and happier one." Instead of saying, "I don't know whether I can go through this; one day is worse than the next," you can say, "I'm turning my life in a whole new direction."

Your children aren't "the poor children"; they are the same

wonderful children they were the day *before* the decision to get a divorce was made. They, too, are up to the challenge of divorce and will find their own new strengths in the process.

Consciously rephrasing the way you've been taught to talk about divorce may feel awkward at first. It's new, and anything new feels a little awkward. The more positive words may grate against ingrained negative attitudes, but they will help bring those negative attitudes to the surface so that they can be transformed into positive ones.

If you "fake it 'til you make it" and use more positive language even before you feel entirely comfortable with it, you will find that your negative attitudes turn around more quickly and that *you soon begin to believe yourself*.

This is true not just for language, but for all your thoughts. It may feel awkward or silly at first; you may think you're acting like Pollyanna. You don't have to go overboard, but stick with it. If positive attitudes aren't a habit for you, it will take some practice. The ability to turn negative into positive is one of the most valuable and rewarding skills you'll ever learn.

SUMMARY

- The divorce hangover's negative attitudes and behaviors are self-destructive, hold you in the past, and sabotage your future.

- It takes an active decision to stop these behaviors and attitudes and to replace them with positive thoughts and actions.

◆

WORKBOOK EXERCISES

◆

1. Make a list of the negative attitudes you have about divorce in general and your divorce in particular.

2. What negative thoughts do you repeat over and over in your mind? How do they make you feel and what behaviors do they cause?

3. Make a list of positive plans and decisions to fill the void left by the negative attitudes. Use upbeat language and notice how it makes you feel.

4. Practice your "new" language when talking to yourself and others.

STEP **10** ◇   ◇   ◇   ◇   ◇   ◇

Rebuild Your Self-Esteem

Self-esteem takes a beating during a divorce, and a divorce hangover does nothing to improve the situation.

When you get married, everybody gathers around to give you gifts and celebrate the dream of living "happily ever after." When you get divorced, people often pull away in disapproval or pity. Instead of getting presents, you *lose* things—everything from the blender, to the house, to the person you thought was the love of your life.

It's no wonder that you lose some self-esteem and confidence along the way. Rebuilding self-esteem is an essential part of the healing process.

12 PRACTICAL STRATEGIES

These are some strategies that my clients and I have found helpful in rebuilding self-esteem:

1. *Create a new vision of yourself.* This is a good time to take a long, hard look at what you want to change about yourself—both inside and out. How would you like to be, to look, and to feel in this new time? Spend some time imagining the "new you" and doing the workbook exercise designed to help you create this vision.

   Some of this work has already been done. Even if you haven't set out consciously to change, you have begun the process by learning about your divorce hangover. You may not recognize the growth yet, but it is there. You'll be pleasantly surprised when you spend some quiet time with yourself and discover the person you've become. Make the break from the person you were and the habits you formed in the old relationship that no longer fit who you are now. Revel in the changes.

2. *Put yourself first.* This is a treacherous and vulnerable time. You are dealing with powerful emotions and attitudes that have been in place for months or years. You are making important decisions and major shifts in attitude. Be gentle with yourself and do things that make you feel good about yourself. Right now, your first priority has to be your own well-being. You may have to care for the kids and/or go to work, but you won't do a good job if you're not also taking care of yourself.

   Get plenty of rest and exercise. Eat well. Get a massage. Give yourself more physical care than you might normally.

   After my divorce, my natural slimness turned to skin and bone. At that point in my life I could eat an elephant and not gain an ounce. To combat my alarming boniness, I began to dance each night before I went to bed. I started to develop some muscle tone and work off all the nervous energy that had accumulated during the day. This became a nightly ritual that left me exhausted and ready to sleep.

3. *Remember you're human.* We all do the best we can, but nobody is perfect and neither is life. Life is growth, and growth often involves struggle and crisis. Once you accept that, and release yourself from the obligation to be perfect, you can relax and just do what needs to be done.

There is no perfect way to heal a divorce hangover. You simply have to do the best you can, one step at a time, relax when you can, and trust yourself and your process.

4. *Be careful how you spend your time.* Do what needs to be done, but make time for you. Stay busy enough that you don't brood or lose yourself in negative thinking, but remember that managing your time effectively doesn't mean filling every minute. Find the balance that works for you between rest and action, physical and emotional activities, work and leisure.

Do all the things you didn't do when you were in your marriage: read a book you've always wanted to read, take a walk, go to a movie, lose yourself in a hobby.

Practice saying no. If someone tries to intrude on your time, simply say, "I'm sorry, I'm working on the aftereffects of my divorce," or "I'm going through a personal crisis." That should scare them off.

5. *Manage your mind chatter.* When you hear your mind begin to chatter or criticize, get up and do something. Change your environment, your position, your activity. Tell your mind to *stop!* Replace those negative thoughts with positive ones.

Steve is an attorney whose mind chatter gets particularly loud right after lunch. "I just couldn't stop thinking about all the things I did wrong, and all the things *she* did wrong. It got so bad I started taking my workbook to the office. Writing this stuff down stops it cold. I see that much of the chatter doesn't make any sense, and that I can't do anything about it anyway. I realize that it's just a waste of time to think about it."

6. *Make changes.* Changes create new energy and new directions. This is a good time to find some new interests, meet new people, change your hair, try a new color, and move the furniture around. Let every change act like a shot in the arm. Remember, these are changes you are *choosing* to make, not changes that have been thrust on you.

Clean the house and empty the drawers if they contain mementos that don't contribute to your self-esteem. I took down all the photos from my first marriage and put them away in albums. The children and I could look at them when we wanted to, but now they weren't a constant reminder in every room of the house.

Be careful not to beat yourself up as you clean house, literally and figuratively. Use this guideline: If something validates you and your self-esteem, keep it. If it doesn't, throw it out or find another place for it.

7. *Seek out people who feel good about you and help you feel good about yourself.* Let yourself be vulnerable and accept help from friends. Let them know you may be calling them for support. We all have to lean on others at some point in life.

This is not the time to have people around you who are needy. You have all you can do to take care of yourself right now, even if it makes you feel good temporarily to take care of someone else.

Remember that others may have their own ideas about what healing your hangover should look like. Some may think that everything between you and your ex-spouse should be sunshine and light now; others may expect you to be miserable and in tears much of the time. These are not the kinds of friends you need right now.

Spend time with people who understand that your needs are volatile, that you may want to talk on the phone for an hour today, but not tomorrow. These people will understand when you do what *you* want to do, and not what they *expect* or *hope* you will do. You may not really want to go on that vacation your mother gave you as a "divorce present."

Choose friends who are genuinely supportive of your strength and well-being, not those who promote victimized attitudes by telling you that you're a "poor thing" or fuel the hangover by being critical of your ex-spouse.

8. *Take risks and give yourself permission to make mistakes.* This is no time to lay low and pull up the drawbridge to your castle. Taking risks and making mistakes are part of life. Embrace them! Bet on a horse, wear a style that is new for you, grow a mustache, take tap dancing lessons, call a friend from grammar school, go out of your way to be nice to someone. It doesn't matter if you make a mistake. That's part of being human. Take the risk just to take the risk, and then you win no matter what the outcome. Do it for yourself, so it doesn't matter what anyone thinks.

9. *Set realistic goals and let these accomplishments feed your self-esteem.* This week you may set a goal of calling your ex-mother-in-law and starting to heal that relationship, cleaning out the spare room, working an hour a day in your divorce hangover workbook, spending some extra time with your children, or breaking one more connection with your ex-spouse. It might not be realistic to set *all* those goals for one week, but keep setting goals and let them move you forward. No matter how small the goal, remember to reward yourself and take that energy into the future.

10. *Keep your sense of humor*. Even if it's gallows humor, allow yourself the gift of laughter. Laughter *is* healing. When you can laugh at how ridiculous a situation is, you not only enjoy temporary relief from the pain, but you release the pent-up tension from all those worries, fears, and bad feelings. Most importantly, you feel renewed, and better able to handle the harsh realities that don't go away.

    After my first postdivorce Christmas, I became almost hysterical laughing when I sat down to figure out how to pay the bills. Yes, I had much less to *pay* with in my new circumstances, but there was much, much less to pay. There were fewer gifts for family members (a whole half of the list had been wiped out!) and half the usual cost of Christmas cards (the attrition rate among my friends had been remarkable!).

    This discovery may not be as funny to everyone as it was to me, but at the time this revelation gave me just the lift I needed. I couldn't feel sorry for myself while I sat there laughing at all my "divorce savings."

    My four-year-old announced one morning during that time, "I don't like all this divorce stuff. Every time I want to watch 'Sesame Street,' you say it's time to go see Dad. Can't I divorce Dad after 'Sesame Street'?!" From the mouths of babes.

11. *Recognize the positive in your marriage*. At some point—perhaps not today, but at some point down the road—you will be able to acknowledge honestly the positive things about your marriage. Even though it didn't last, good things came of it. Search them out and affirm them to yourself.

12. *Reward yourself*. Congratulate yourself at every opportunity. Send yourself flowers. Don't analyze whether or not you deserve them. You *need* them! You deserve as much as you can possibly give yourself just for being alive today and willing to heal your divorce hangover.

    When you've made a decision, avoided falling into a hangover habit, handled a difficult issue with the children, managed to go about your business without the day being dominated by hangover thoughts, or even when there is no good reason . . . give yourself a reward. You may need a reward most on the days when things *aren't* going well.

Often it's hard to think of a reward at the very times when you need one most, so keep a "Rewards List" in your workbook for reference. You might include things like:

- Take a bubble bath
- Go for a walk in the park
- Take yourself to a movie or show
- Send yourself flowers
- Go window shopping
- Have dinner out
- Make a special trip to visit a friend

THE SPIRIT OF GENEROSITY

Practicing the spirit of generosity is another way to rebuild self-esteem. Generosity means giving both yourself and your ex-spouse a break.

When I talk about being generous, I do not mean being a doormat. I don't mean conceding every issue, or trying to please your ex-spouse at the expense of your own needs and wants. I do mean seeing things from his or her point of view as well as your own, trying to be fair, and not succumbing to the temptation to blame or punish. Being generous makes you feel good about yourself.

In the heat of her divorce, Pat had insisted that her ex-husband have minimal visitation rights. He saw the children only about once a month, and never on holidays. Shortly after Pat had started working on her divorce hangover, he called to say that it would mean a lot to him if the kids could spend the Easter holidays with him.

A few months earlier, Pat would have laughed in his face. Now that she was feeling better about herself and not carrying around the bitterness that had surrounded the divorce, she felt more open to discussing it. The kids were very excited about the prospect, and Pat agreed to let them go.

She didn't really lose anything, and she gained gratitude, admiration, and goodwill from both her ex-husband and her children. More importantly, she felt terrific about herself.

ENLIGHTENED SELF-INTEREST

Being generous is not only the right thing to do, it is also in your best interest.

- *You take back control.* Instead of standing by helplessly, you make decisions that are likely to work for all concerned and determine the course of events.
- *You wear the white hat.* You never have to feel guilty, cheap, petty, or mean. You have done the fair thing, perhaps even bent over backward a bit to accommodate the other person, and you can feel proud of that. That is no small achievement.
- *You make the situation less adversarial.* You create an atmosphere of goodwill and good faith between you and your ex-spouse. This is not only good for your mental and emotional well-being, but a good investment if you still share responsibilities in such areas as the children or finances. Any legal contract can be broken; goodwill makes any agreement truly binding.

  Your ex-spouse doesn't have much to push up against if you decide not to resist, and are willing to work together. This often takes people by surprise and can stop a fight before it begins.

  When my first husband and I began talking about divorce, he said, "Well, I guess you expect to have custody of the children." I said, "Absolutely not. I think you and I need to sit down together and decide what's best for them." This defused a lot of his animosity and set the tone for working through other issues.

- *Helping the other person stay free of the divorce hang-*

over helps you to stay free. The hangover is a two-way street. If one party is involved, it's very difficult for the other person to stay out of it. Instead of succumbing to the punch-counterpunch dynamic, you can step back, take a deep breath, remember that the other person is hurting, too, and not escalate the fight.

A LEAP OF FAITH

Adopting the spirit of generosity isn't easy when you first start treating a divorce hangover. All your instincts and habits tell you to do the opposite—to protect, defend, and strike out at the other person. There is no guarantee that everything will work out if you are generous; you simply have to trust that it will. This is a leap of faith.

It may help to ask yourself how well things are working out *now*.

KEEP AT IT

Healing the hangover isn't a matter of simply going through the ten steps in this chapter once. You may work your way down to Number Six and realize you still have work to do on Number Four. Some of the steps will be easy for you; some will be more difficult and require more attention. Stay flexible, and stay vigilant.

◆

SUMMARY

- During and after a divorce, you must consciously rebuild self-esteem.

- Increased self-esteem brings your life back into focus and allows you to take control of your future.

◆

This process can be a springboard to a whole new way of relating to yourself, to other people, and to life. Your success in healing the hangover will give you the skills and confidence to handle anything that comes up.

◆

WORKBOOK EXERCISES
◆

1. Describe how you feel now.

2. Think of several people, real or imagined, whom you admire. List the traits that appeal to you about them.

3. Describe the person you would like to be, based on these traits. Start practicing these qualities.

4. For each of the twelve strategies, list an action you will take to start rebuilding your self-esteem.

MANAGING YOUR WORLD
AND KEEPING
THE HANGOVER AT BAY

◇

5

Power: Understanding and Using It Effectively

◇

There must be . . . a community of power;
nor organized rivalries but an organized
common peace.

—WOODROW WILSON,
SPEECH BEFORE THE SENATE

◇

As you heal the divorce hangover, your relationships with people change. You are more confident and at peace with yourself, clearer about what you want, and more likely to be generous. All these things will be reflected in the way you use power—the most basic element in any human relationship.

Power is a neutral energy; it can be used positively or negatively—handled with grace, or badly abused. Before you go back into the world and start relating to others in your new, posthangover state, it's important to know how you used power in the past, how you are handling it now, and what you want to do with it in the future.

87

Balance of Power

Who calls the shots, and in which areas? This question tells you more about a relationship than any other. Most relationships come apart because there is an imbalance or misuse of power.

The ideal marriage is a partnership. Power is shared equally through a process of joint decision-making in which both people feel valued, responsible, and appreciated for their contributions.

This breaks down when either:

1. *Someone abdicates power.* ("Oh, do it *your* way!" "Why ask me? You always get what you want anyway!")

or

2. *Someone seizes all the power without thinking of others' needs.* ("Don't ask questions now; let me handle this!" "Stay out of the way. I'll explain later.")

These same people may soon be asking, "When do I get to be a part of what's going on?" or "Why do I always have to decide everything?" Both modes cause resentment and set the stage for future trouble.

Power and the Hangover

The struggles you experience during and after divorce are essentially power struggles.

Do you still have fights or resentments about who got the TV? Who got which friends? Custody or visitation rights? The financial settlement? *If you are still trying to leverage power in any area, or allowing yourself to be leveraged, you are still bound to the other person.* This is the energy that fuels the hangover.

Power issues that aren't resolved during the marriage (and most aren't, or the marriage would remain intact) are carried into the divorce. If they aren't resolved in the divorce, they become the glue that holds the hangover together.

8 "Power Points"

"Power points" are areas where power issues are likely to surface. Knowing where your "power points" are can help you heal past hurts, stay clear of problems that trigger your hangover, and make good decisions about your current relationship and your future.

Imbalances of power usually start in early courtship. Minor problems become larger ones in the marriage, huge stumbling blocks in the divorce, and walls of granite in the hangover.

Sometimes power issues begin even earlier, in childhood. You may have made unconscious decisions about power by watching how your parents used or abused it, shared or hoarded it, and by how they treated you.

As you read through this list of "power points," ask yourself: how your parents handled these issues, how you felt about how they handled them, and how you handle them as an adult. Be alert to the areas in which you have felt abused or abusive:

1. *Finances.* Who controls the money? This is the acid test of whether the relationship is a partnership or a solo show. Kathy loved Rob when they got married, but she was also relieved to be out of the woods financially. His success as a real estate developer meant she could quit her nursing job and would have the leisure and backing to set up a home care service someday. She was so delighted with this prospect that she abdicated almost all control in the financial area and let Rob make all the monetary decisions.

   When they were divorced five years later, Rob and his lawyer wrote up the financial settlement and presented it to Kathy as a *fait accompli.* She was stunned that he hadn't even consulted her about her needs. The settlement was generous—perhaps even more than she would have demanded—but she still felt powerless and pushed aside. It doesn't matter how generously financial power is wielded; if that power is not shared, one person feels diminished and resentful.

In the ten years that they were married, Winnie and Walter kept sweeping the uncomfortable money issue under the rug. He was the sole breadwinner and never dealt with his resentment about this. She never dealt with her guilt.

After the divorce, Winnie wanted the settlement in one lump sum so that it would be *over*. He insisted that it be doled out on a monthly basis "so she'll remember where it's coming from and that she couldn't make it on her own." He liked the fact that she had to stay in his good graces in order to keep getting the checks and had to wonder each month if the payment would be on time. He abused his financial power in order to keep their connection alive, and she allowed it to happen.

When the size of the paycheck dictates who holds power, the other person may feel obliged to give ground in other areas—sex, household maintenance, time, etc.—or else do just the opposite, leverage these other areas of power to "even the score." This dynamic dehumanizes the person who feels that he or she must "pay," or exact payment, in order to make up for not bringing in as much money. The equilibrium is out of whack and trouble is sure to follow.

Sharing monetary power supports everyone's psychological well-being. It is also easier to keep to a budget, plan for large purchases (house, appliances, vacations), contribute to savings, and make investments when both people have participated in making these decisions.

2. *Children*. Traditionally, women have held more power in this area. Most women still have custody of the children, even though this is no longer a foregone conclusion. They usually have more contact with them, more influ-

ence over them, and more control of the time their fathers spend with them. When women need a weapon against men's traditional power in the financial arena, they usually look to the children.

Beth and Howard got caught in a classic chess game, with money and the children as pawns. Howard had always paid child support, but it had been ten years since the divorce, the children were fifteen and sixteen and no longer needed Beth at home, and he felt she should be "out there working at something, *anything*, so she could start taking care of herself" and he could stop paying alimony.

Beth didn't like to admit it, but she was afraid to go back to work. She had been employed briefly as a secretary in an insurance office before the children were born, and she knew she didn't want to go back to that. She hadn't enjoyed it and wasn't even sure she could handle it at this point. Rather than deal directly with her fears, she fought back at Howard by making it extremely difficult for him to see the children. She also told the children that he was threatening to withdraw alimony and possibly even child support, and that she wasn't at all sure that they could go to college now. They rallied around her and made him the bad guy, which so enraged Howard that he actually did stop sending alimony checks and Beth had to pay everything out of the child support money.

"I was grasping at straws," she said, "determined to fight back with the only weapons I had, and unfortunately, those were my children."

Finally, the situation became so extreme that they sought therapy. In these sessions, Beth understood that she was only hurting herself by giving in to her fears about working. She began career counseling, worked up her courage to start going on interviews, and began to follow the career plan that she and the counselor had developed.

Howard realized that arbitrarily withholding alimony

checks was neither fair nor productive. They were able to sit down and work out a plan for him to gradually reduce these payments as Beth became more independent. She felt better about herself and stopped berating Howard to the children.

3. *Time*. Some people have a high need for "time off" to be by themselves. Others want more contact and feel left out when their partners go off by themselves. If couples work out a plan so that everyone's needs are met, time won't be used as a weapon.

Mark liked quiet time at home and balked when Julie announced that they were having two dinner parties that week. She reminded him that he had spent all of Saturday and half of Sunday playing golf. She felt "cheated" out of this time with him and reacted by unilaterally scheduling more social time.

When Moira said she would rather stay home than go with Ethan and the kids to the park, he reminded her that she had spent three nights out that week—two with her women friends and one at a political function—and implied that she was not a good mother.

In both cases, the dynamic of "You did this, so I get to do that!" continued into the divorces and hangovers. Julie said to Mark, "If you'd had time to meet with my lawyer before the divorce, I wouldn't have to take you back to court now." Ethan got custody of the children and was always saying to Moira, "You never had time for them *then*. Why should I let you see them now?"

4. *Sex*. Sex can be an extremely vulnerable area. Misusing sexual power is one of the quickest ways to damage a relationship. When power is abused in this area, the scars can be deep.

Withholding sex, demanding sex, trading sex, or using sex in any way except to share and enjoy physical intimacy undermines this deep and powerful part of any relationship.

In the last troubled days of their marriage, Jordan

punished Noreen by withholding sex despite their strong attraction for one another. They fought like pit bulls in their frequent court appearances during the divorce, but her greatest pleasure in life was seducing him afterward. He couldn't resist and she loved the power this gave her. Whatever she might have lost in court, or in the marriage, she felt she won back in the bedroom.

5. *Home.* Home is another area that has traditionally been managed by women, although men may be beginning to take more responsibility for household chores and the family's emotional climate.

Terri held such tight control over the refrigerator that her three children had to get specific permission ("in triplicate," they half-joked) to remove anything. This was inconvenient for everyone, but Terri had so little power elsewhere in her family that she clung desperately to this one area, claiming, "How can I feed all of you when I never know what's in the refrigerator?"

Spouses who feel powerless over too many areas of their marriage, who have very little voice in decision-making, will often act out their anger or frustration in the home "arena." One woman habitually "forgot" to launder her husband's shirts, while another kept her house so immaculate and ordered that her husband was unable to relax and feel at home.

6. *Social life.* Some people are more social than others. They enjoy going out and mix easily with friends or strangers. Others are happier staying home, or doing informal, low-key entertaining. They are inclined to be quiet in a group, and shy with strangers.

Again, partners can be very different and yet compatible if both people understand and respect one another's needs. The trouble arises when one or both parties use social situations to play out their power struggle.

Lucy was painfully shy, and Claude forced her beyond her comfort level at parties. He pushed her forward, asked her pointed questions, and set her up to tell stories. She would have preferred to listen quietly, but he wanted a wife who was more social.

7. *Religion.* Religion involves our most fundamental beliefs and can arouse some of our deepest feelings. People have often decided not to marry because of differences in religion. Although this is not as common as it once was, everyone needs to feel that his or her religious beliefs are respected, even if they are not shared. This is equally true of political philosophies.

8. *Privacy and personal habits.* Personal habits involve the real basics: how the other person eats, personal hygiene, bathroom behaviors, etc. I know a woman who says she divorced her husband because of the way he chewed in fast little bites, just like a rabbit. Another marriage was saved because the couple decided to use separate bathrooms.

Whenever Barry gets upset with Toni, all he can think about is how she wore too much makeup. Their marriage didn't break up because of her iridescent eye shadow or mauve blush, but these things always bothered him. They stuck in his mind and became a catalyst for other resentments.

Power Pioneers

The way we've been using power has not worked. Because men have traditionally held the financial power, and women have held power in the area of home and children, these are the most common weapons used to leverage power. Not only is it destructive to use these important aspects of life as weapons, but the whole idea of needing to manipulate and leverage power keeps everybody stuck in a dehumanizing and counterproductive battle.

To make our relationships successful, nurturing, and lasting, *we have to start doing things differently*. We have to let go of antiquated attitudes and power structures. We have to tell the truth about what we want. We have to become pioneers and find new ways of *sharing* power, rather than *fighting over* it or *misusing* it to get what we want.

No one wants to feel abused or abusive. We all want to be loved and honored, and to love and honor our partners. Beneath all the smokescreens and confusion that surround it, *true power comes from feeling recognized, appreciated, and respected.* An equal sharing of power means, first and foremost, joint decisions in an atmosphere of mutual recognition, appreciation, and respect.

Men and women have to allow each other to be fully human, equal partners, and discover the rewards of sharing power even in their last bastion—finances. Women have to stop expecting men to take care of them and demanding special consideration because they feel weak or inept. They have to find their own strengths, both emotionally and financially.

Seizing Power, Kindly

If you were the "victim," healing the hangover means reclaiming your power. Seize back the control in your life, but do it kindly. Don't give in to the temptation to exploit those who have exploited you. It's not worth the cost to your self-esteem. Now is not the time to get it all back, or to even the score. This just keeps you engaged in the struggle. Make sure your needs are met, but let the rest go so that you can establish yourself as a separate entity and prepare yourself for future relationships.

Anita had been moping around for three years, bitter about her "paltry" financial settlement and how her ex-husband had "stolen the best years of her life." A visit from her sister, who had risen above a similar situation, inspired her to action.

She figured out exactly what she needed to live comfortably and designed a plan to earn that amount by expanding her part-time bookkeeping work. She joined a local tennis association and a church where she was likely to meet people. Anita seized back the power in her life not by retaliating against her ex-husband, but by expanding her own horizons. This gave her more choices, more freedom, and far greater control than going after him would have brought her.

If you were the one who abused power, healing will come by giving some of it back. True power stems from appreciation and respect for yourself that you extend to those around you.

Even if your lives are no longer connected by money or children and you never see one another, you can heal the situation by changing your attitude toward the other person and at least stop thinking about him or her so negatively. If you do have contact, you can start treating him or her differently and offering to share the power that you once hoarded.

Frances and Dean decided that both they and the children would be better off if they stopped abusing their respective areas of power. He agreed to stop sending child support checks two weeks late and she agreed to abide by the legal visitation rights, rather than retaliating for the late checks by announcing when he showed up Friday afternoon that the children were spending the weekend with their grandparents. As a bonus to herself, Frances also decided to stop being so critical of him in front of the children.

The 4 Healing Steps

Resolving the power struggle in your hangover keeps you from taking the anger or frustration out on your family, friends, and children—or carrying it over into your next relationship. It involves four basic steps:

1. *Notice the areas in which you and/or your ex-spouse abused, or continue to abuse, power.* Did the power struggles have to do with money? Sex? Family? Time? Household responsibilities? Children? All of the above? What else? When you catch yourself moving unconsciously into the old pattern—whether abused or abusive—stop and ask yourself if this is what you really want to do.

2. *Detach from the power struggle with your ex-spouse.* It only feeds your hangover and prevents you from getting on with your life. Your goal is separation and emotional distance, not hand-to-hand combat. Competition has no place in healing the hangover. Don't give the other person the power to throw your life into chaos.

   If he or she wants the TV and simply will not let the issue die, it may be better just to give it back. If the two of you have been engaged in a battle of words over your friends' loyalties, letting go of the struggle will not only make you feel better, but will make your friends feel more comfortable around you.

3. *Work toward an equilibrium of power* in the areas where your lives still overlap. If you are using children or money as pawns in your power struggle, for instance, talk with your ex-spouse about ways to stop. Do what you can to establish an atmosphere of trust and respect.

   - *If you've been fighting* for more money or more time with the children, figure out what you absolutely need in these areas, sit down with your ex-spouse, show your goodwill, and try to work something out. Put these issues to rest. You may not get what you originally wanted—everyone may have to give a little—but it will be something and you'll be at peace. Most importantly, you will have worked toward resolving the issues *together.*

   - *If you were the abusive one,* give back some of the power so that you are closer to an equal partnership. You may even want to let your ex-spouse know that you're doing this, and acknowledge that you've abused your power in the past.

   - *If you were abused,* tell the truth about what happened and then let go of it. For your own sake, forgive the other person. Then forgive yourself for allowing him or her to abuse you. You can't move forward without doing this.

4. *Remember the spirit of generosity.* Your purpose is not justice or retribution, but healing. Try to consider both your own and the other person's needs. Give a little more than you have to. It will do wonders for your self-esteem, and the other person may even start being more generous, too.

Power Sharing

Every relationship has to find its own balance of power and its own way of sharing decisions. You don't have to agree on everything, but you do have to be able to talk about issues and arrive together at ways to handle them.

If each person feels heard and understood, then there is almost nothing that can't be worked out. In this kind of partnership, each partner is a whole person and chooses to be with the other from love and commitment, rather than from fear or dependency.

One way to guarantee that your next relationship or marriage will thrive is to practice this kind of power-sharing with

---

SUMMARY

• Abuse, misuse, and imbalance of power play fundamental roles in the breakdown of relationships.

• Unresolved power struggles feed the divorce hangover.

• Power issues often show up around the eight "power points" of finances, children, time, sex, home, social life, religion, and privacy and personal habits.

• Marriage and divorce are shared responsibilities.

your ex-spouse. If you can pull that off, you can probably establish an equal relationship with anybody. The added benefit is that your life will be a lot easier.

◆

WORKBOOK EXERCISES

◆

1. Did you and your partner share equal responsibility during your marriage and divorce?

2. Write down the eight "power points" and any others that were important in your marriage or divorce, and give examples of each.

3. Who was the abuser of power in each area? Who was the abused?

4. Which behaviors bothered you the most and caused the most conflict between you—during the marriage, during the divorce, and afterward?

• 6 •

Children and the Divorce Hangover

◇

You may give them your love but not your
    thoughts
for they have their own thoughts.
You may house their bodies but not their souls
for their souls dwell in the house of tomorrow
which you cannot visit, not even in your
    dreams.
Seek not to make them like you
for life goes not backward nor tarries with
    yesterday.

—KAHLIL GIBRAN,
THE PROPHET

◇

Children's Divorce Hangovers Are Different

When children see the family breaking apart, they don't know
what's going on, and their survival is threatened on two deep
and primitive levels:

1. **Safety:** *The physical environment* that is supposed to
   protect and nurture them seems to be at risk. "Home"

isn't the way it was. At the very least, Daddy isn't at breakfast. In the chaos and confusion, they may not even be sure that they'll have a place to live.

2. **Love**: *The emotional environment* they need to feel secure and worthwhile seems to be falling apart. Children need to know absolutely that both parents will always love them, no matter what. Now they're afraid that the parent who left has already stopped loving them. If that person can stop loving them, so can the other parent. If the parents can stop loving one another, they can stop loving their children.

These are deep survival fears, and such fears are at the root of children's hangovers, just as anger is at the root of ours. Every aspect of their lives seems to be in jeopardy, and the result is a pervasive terror. They need clear, honest answers—fast—to avoid a hangover.

FEAR: THE CORE EMOTION

April was seven when her parents got divorced, and they were terrified that it would ruin her life. They were afraid to talk about it, glossed over her questions, tried to pretend that nothing was happening, and were jumpy whenever she was around.

April sensed all this mental hand-wringing, but whenever she asked what was going on, her mother just said, "Everything's going to be fine, honey." The message April received was, "Don't ask any more questions. It's so terrible that I don't even want to talk about it."

The more mixed messages April got, the more confused and frightened she became. She didn't know if her father still loved her. He had moved out of the house—perhaps because of something she did—and she didn't know when, or if, she would see him again. She had spent the weekend that he left with her grandmother, who kept eyeing her pitifully and saying, "You poor dear."

April had heard arguments about whether or not she and

her mother could continue to live in the house, and so she wasn't sure she would be starting back to the same school in September. She wasn't even sure they would have a roof over their heads. Her neighborhood friends asked her about what was happening (perhaps prompted by *their* parents), and she was embarrassed not to know much more than they did.

Everything was changing and she didn't know what would happen next. Her mother might not love her either, and might take off at any moment. Then where would she live? How would she eat? Why didn't they love her? What had she done? There seemed to be no answers and no more guarantees in life.

April's terrors and uncertainties mushroomed. The only way she could cope was to shut down and not feel anything. She became a blank-eyed little girl who showed very little interest in her world and awoke screaming each night from nightmares.

CHILDREN'S LOSSES AND CHANGES

In the midst of a divorce, nothing in a child's life is predictable. The whole world is on shaky ground and they can't count on anything. Each child has his or her own questions and fears, even if he or she can't verbalize them. These are some common ones:

- Does the parent who left still love me? Will I see him or her again? When and how often?
- Will the other parent stay with me, or will he or she leave, too? Does this parent still love me?
- If the parents stopped loving one another, why wouldn't they stop loving me?
- Was the divorce my fault?
- Were will we live?
- Will we have enough money?
- Will I keep going to the same school?
- What else is going to change in my environment? Have I lost everything I'm going to lose, or will there be more losses and changes down the road?
- How will this affect my future?

The sooner you tell your children exactly what is happening, reassure them that they will be safe and cared for, and let them know in no uncertain terms that both of their parents will always love them, the better off they will be. If you step in immediately with this *information* and *reassurance*, you can stop a hangover dead in its tracks. Children are amazingly resilient and pragmatic in a crisis. If they know that they are loved, that they are safe, and how the changes will affect their day-to-day lives, then they can deal with almost anything.

NIGHTMARES AND DEMONS

When children don't get their questions answered and their fears calmed with direct, accurate, complete information, they panic and start making up their own answers. *This is when the hangover starts.* Their imagination moves with blinding speed and power. Real, specific fears balloon into an enormous, amorphous ball of fear that touches every aspect of their lives. They no longer fear just specific losses and changes; they simply *fear*— everything. Soon the whole drama is being played out *not around their real fears, but around their imaginary fears.*

As in an adult's hangover, the initial core emotion—in this case, fear—is redirected toward something other than its true source.

- Anthony, 5, refused to go to sleep unless the closet door was open and he could see before the lights went out that there were no monsters inside.
- Marsha, 8, refused to ride in the car with their neighbor, who had come to pick her up and take her to her grandmother's house the weekend her father left.
- Alec, 10, started clinging to his mother and wouldn't leave the house without her, afraid that she wouldn't be there when he came back.
- Donna, 14, refused to meet new friends in the town to which they moved. She said they'd just have to move again if she got close to anyone.
- Holly, 16, developed a frightening set of beliefs and at-

titudes about the horrors of relationships after her father physically assaulted her mother and left them permanently.

This once-removed fear can also manifest itself as anger, but in children's hangovers, anger always emerges *after* the initial trauma, after they realize that they aren't getting answers or reassurances from you. This anger may show up as sullenness, a refusal to talk, or a defiant attitude of "You can't tell *me* what to do!"

THE ANTIDOTES: LOVE AND TRUTH

It is very easy to make children feel secure. *All you have to do is tell them the truth and make sure they know you love them.* This applies whether you are in the process of divorce now, or working with your children on hangovers. If their hangovers have been in place for a long time, you may need to be more patient, but love and honesty are still the keys. Because they couldn't stand to see him in pain, Ben's parents told him that they were going to try and work things out, that they might get back together. When two months passed without their having any contact, Ben turned sullen and withdrawn. His conversation became monosyllabic and he wouldn't look at his mother, with whom he lived.

He knew they'd lied to him, and that was yet another loss. He could no longer trust them to tell him the truth.

When you tell your children what is happening, or what happened, during the divorce, don't let your own emotions get in the way. If you can't get a grip on yourself, don't have that talk yet. The focus should be on *them,* not on you. It is your job to comfort your children, not the other way around. Their hugs and nearness will be comforting, of course, but don't make that their job.

If you are talking to your children at the time of the divorce, don't shy away from the truth. If Mommy or Daddy has gone away permanently, tell them that's what has happened even if it is their worst fear. They have to know what their reality is. Let them know that you are absolutely *not* going away, that you are going to be there for them forever. You need to establish a rock-bottom level of safety for them, a point beyond which there will be no more losses or changes.

In an attempt to return to normalcy as quickly as possible, some parents gloss over their children's questions and confusion about all the changes in their lives. You do need to establish some normalcy in the children's lives. They have to know where their teddy bear is, that their clothes are hanging in the closet for school tomorrow, that there is going to be a bedtime story. These supportive structures and routines help everybody, but honesty shouldn't be sacrificed for normalcy.

When children feel part of what is going on and trusted with information, they begin to believe that there may be a future after all, that they will be safe and that eventually everyone will be okay. The circumstances may change—you may have less money or have to move—but *the love will be there, and they will be safe*.

If years have passed since your divorce and you weren't in a position to give them this kind of attention at that time, *it is not too late*. You can apply the same principles now.

WHAT TO TELL YOUR CHILDREN: 11 GUIDELINES

These are guidelines for working with children during the actual divorce. If you are dealing with a hangover, read them over to see where you or your children may have missed a step. This will help you pinpoint potential problems and guide your talks with them later on.

1. Once you and your spouse have decided to get a divorce, tell the children as soon as possible, but be sure you put your emotional turmoil on the back burner, at first.
2. It is less important which of you tells them than it is for the two of you to discuss beforehand how and what you are going to say.
3. Whether you decide to tell them together or separately,

give the children a chance early in this process to discuss the divorce with each of you.

4. Emphasize that the divorce is between the two of you, and is in no way their fault.

5. Let them know that you both love them, and that this is not going to change.

6. Anticipate any questions you think they may ask so that the two of you can discuss how you want to answer them. The news of your divorce probably won't take them completely by surprise.

7. Do not lay out all the inevitable changes right at the beginning. Children usually need time to digest this first big change—the divorce itself—before they can handle the others.

8. If they do ask specific questions about other changes, don't put them off, thinking that they are not ready. If they are asking the questions, they are ready to hear the answers. By getting these answers, they can begin to make adjustments and come to grips with their circumstances.

9. If you and your spouse have not discussed a question that the children bring up, don't blurt out an answer before the two of you have had a chance to discuss it in private. Tell the children that you have to talk about it first, and will let them know the answer as soon as you have decided. Don't put them off with "I don't know," or "We'll talk about it later." Instead, say, "We haven't talked about that yet, but it's important to all of us. The two of us will discuss it, then we'll all talk about it as a group. Until then, everything will be the same as it always has been."

10. Include the children, but never make them responsible for decisions. You, the parents, are responsible for making all decisions. You can bring them into the discussion with questions like "We're going to have to move." "How do you feel about moving?" "How do you like this house or that house?" "What kind of house

would you like to live in?" But never abdicate the leadership role.

Children need for *someone* to be the leader and decision-maker. If parents don't assume this role, children will take it on. When children are handed this inappropriate level of responsibility, a primitive fear is triggered. They know somehow that things are upside down and that this is not their natural role. In their simple wisdom, they are afraid of this power because they know that they aren't capable of wielding it well. Even children who have the intelligence and determination to pull it off, or who have an aura of maturity and stability about them, pay a high emotional price.

11. Accept whatever your children need to do in order to get through this crisis. Don't stifle their feelings or tell them to grieve more or less than they are. If they have to engage in inappropriate behaviors, like spilling their milk on the floor over and over, allow them to do that. You don't have to clean it up yourself each time, but you do have to find the strength and emotional distance to say to yourself, "Okay, this is what Johnny has to do right now." Then have them get down and help you clean it up. Try to talk with Johnny about what is happening. You might begin with something like, "Are you upset or nervous? You seem a little clumsy and that's not like you." Try to get them to talk about what is bothering them.

Again, the whole idea behind these guidelines is to help your children feel secure and loved.

The Symptoms of Children's Hangovers

How can you spot your children's hangovers and what can you do about them?

The symptoms of children's hangovers are usually anxiety

symptoms. You may see thumb-sucking, teeth-grinding, bed-wetting, general agitation, or withdrawal, depending on the children's ages.

Some symptomatic behaviors are:

BODY LANGUAGE

- They don't look or feel relaxed, and are sometimes tense to the point that their bodies are huddled over on themselves.
- They turn their heads away or look down when the subject of the other parent comes up. Even such innocent questions as "Did you have a good time?" may prompt this kind of reaction. This is a natural, supportive interest and shouldn't make them uncomfortable. It is different from the sort of third-degree questions that *should* prompt an uncomfortable response from children: "What sort of food did you eat? Did he dress you warmly? Who did you meet when you were with him?"

VERBAL SIGNALS

- They refuse to talk at all about the other parent, or seem to be withholding whenever he or she is mentioned.
- They regularly change the subject when the other parent comes up in conversation.
- They give mumbled or monosyllabic responses ("Yes," "No," "I don't know") to questions about the other parent. This is a defense mechanism, a way to avoid a subject that is painful to them.

ESCAPE

- They disappear into their rooms, spend hours watching television, jump at the chance to get out of the house, and in some cases get involved with substance or behavioral addictions—drugs, alcohol, overeating, undereating, shoplifting, or promiscuity.

- They may even walk away when you are talking to them, especially if the subject is their other parent and they are uncomfortable about the way the two of you are relating.

ACTING OUT

This can take the form of tantrums, hysterical reactions, fainting, general recalcitrance, or antisocial behavior. They can act out toward either parent, in school, with friends, or with strangers.

Cathy, 8, had always manipulated her parents by throwing hysterical fits and then fainting. Their divorce simply gave her a larger, more dramatic context in which to play out this game of control. As bad as her behavior had been, it got worse. The same behavior worked for her before. After the divorce, she just turned up the volume.

One evening Cathy, her younger brother, her father, and her father's new wife arrived at a party. She was so upset that she refused to go in. Not only that, but she enlisted her little brother's support and the two of them sat out in the freezing cold while the adults attended the party. Cathy was willing to go to any lengths to assert her control.

This kind of behavior is infuriating, but it was Cathy's only way of coping with what was, to her, an unacceptable situation. At least it got people's attention; she no longer felt ignored and swept under the carpet, as she had during the divorce.

When you see a pattern of these kinds of behaviors over a period of time (once is not enough), realize that your child is crying out for help and bring a counselor into the picture. Except in very rare cases, this behavior will not go away by itself. It may take other forms, but the basic ingredients will remain the same. You and your child have to get the help you need.

The Hangover That Children "Catch" from a Parent

Many children emerge from divorce without hangovers—either because their parents handled the situation well or because they are resilient. It is possible, however, for children to "catch" a hangover later on from one of their parents, which mirrors the parent's hangover.

Debby and Sean were six and nine when their parents divorced, and they lived with their mother. Neither appeared to have a hangover until about four years later, when their parents' relationship again became difficult because of a revision in the financial settlement. At that point, their father's carefully hidden hangover flared into full-blown antagonism.

Their mother began to notice changes in Sean after he and his sister had visited their father. He wouldn't look at her when he talked about his father, his body language was very closed, and he began to treat her with exactly the same brand of sarcasm that her ex-husband always used.

Debby, who was more direct, told her mother that her father had become quite critical and sarcastic about the mother's "money-grubbing" attitude. But she had also told her dad that she didn't like hearing mean things about her mother. Because she was able to talk to both parents about her feelings, Debby never did develop much of a hangover.

Whenever Sean's mother tried to talk to him about his obvious internal struggle, it seemed to her that he turned into a junior version of his father and shut down. Finally she realized that she was only making matters worse by trying to force him to talk about things that he was clearly not ready to discuss, and decided just to let him be where he was for now, trust the loving way she had worked with him during the divorce itself, and wait for him to come around.

At some point when she feels he is ready to hear it, she may say something like, "I think there have been times in your life when the feelings your father has about me have been difficult for you, and I understand. I'd like to talk about that if you feel comfortable with it." You may have to create these opportunities for children over and over again. Be patient; when they are ready, they will open up.

Hangover Flare-ups

When are your children's hangovers most likely to flare up? This depends on the kind of hangover they have.

If the hangover results from their own unresolved fears and confusion, it can show up just about anywhere. Over time, you will begin to see a pattern. It may flare up each time they have to take a trip out of town, because that reminds them of when they stayed with a relative or friend during the divorce. It may flare up when they see the color blue, because that is what they were wearing or looking at when they found out about the divorce. Be alert and question them about anything that seems strange to you, anything that makes you think, "That's not like Susie."

If your children "caught" a hangover from you or your ex-spouse, it is likely to flare up over the same issues.

Noah's father was always telling him, "I think it's terrible that your mother goes out so much. She should be home taking care of you instead of leaving you with a sitter. Who knows who that babysitter is, anyway?"

When Noah sees his mother getting ready to go out, he whines, "I want you to stay home with me. Why are you going out again? I need you."

Leanne lives with her father during the week and her mother on weekends. Her father always insists on having brown bread in the house and won't tolerate white bread. Her mother does just the opposite, partly in resistance to her ex-husband. When Leanne goes to her mother's house on weekends, she absolutely refuses to eat the white bread. She is playing out the clash between her parents, asserting some control against her mother (*"No! I won't eat that!)* and at the same time gets the payoff of being "Daddy's good little girl" because she is doing something her father would like.

Children's hangovers can also flare up around issues with their parents' new spouses. The new spouses may have different points of view from what the children are used to, or different ways of doing things. They may always eat dinner at 7:00 rather than at 6:00, sleep late on Sunday morning instead of having everyone up at 8:00 for church or an outing, or do any number of things that seem strange and not so wonderful to the children—either because they have to get used to something new or because they feel jealous or threatened.

Find positive ways to present these new spouses and new regimes to your children, rather than seeing them as potential problems. I think children are lucky to be exposed to different points of view. Open their eyes to their new opportunities. For example, now they have two Christmases, two birthdays, two homes, and double the number of people to love and care about them.

8 Steps to Help Your Children Heal Their Hangovers

Remember, it is never too late to go back and deal with something that was not handled in the heat or confusion of the divorce. Just because you didn't discuss it then doesn't mean you can't talk about it now.

If you weren't able to follow the eleven guidelines at the time of your divorce, or if your children now have hangovers, these are some steps you can take to help them heal:

1. *Schedule time to sit down with your children and ask them:*

   • How they feel about the divorce
   • How they feel about their relationships with you, with their other parent, with any new spouses who may be present, and with their new siblings, if any
   • How they feel about the relationship between you and your ex-spouse

2. *Ask them about their fears and confusion* at the time of the divorce, and hear what they have to say. If they draw

a blank, encourage them to think about it more. They *were* frightened and confused, and it is healthy for them to understand what those fears and confusions were. The sooner they can say, "Oh, *that's* why I was so confused and frightened . . . ," the sooner they can let go.

3. *If they ask, tell the truth about how you were feeling* then and how you are feeling now about the divorce. Don't be afraid to be honest with them. If you are still working hard on some aspects of your hangover, it's okay to tell them that, as long as you don't dump on them or expect them to fix it for you.

   It is a terrible strain to have perfect parents, and sometimes letting them see your vulnerabilities creates more closeness. This is a wonderful opportunity to deepen and enrich your relationship with them.

4. *Make it safe for them to express and come to grips with any leftover bad feelings or unresolved emotions.* If Amy is still angry with you or your ex-spouse, she needs to be able to tell you that. If Brad still thinks you are a bad parent, he needs the freedom to express that opinion.

   When children can't tell you these things, it is hard for them to let go. When the two of you can talk about their feelings and opinions, and everything can be aired openly, then the negativity can be released rather than festering in the darkness.

5. *Accept them exactly the way they are today,* with whatever feelings or behaviors they are exhibiting. Don't tell them what they should have been feeling at the time of the divorce, or what they should be doing or feeling now. If they are still sad or upset, don't try to *change* their feelings; instead, let them talk, hear what they say, and find out how you can support them in releasing those unresolved emotions.

6. *Offer to loan them this book, but don't force it down their throats.*

7. *Offer them outside help*. If you feel they need more help than you can give them—either because you are still involved in your own hangover or because their problems are beyond your ability to cope—then make sure they get that support from a therapist, counselor, or other professional.

   It will be valuable for you to sit in on some of these sessions. It may be easier for your children to tell you some things with a third person present. They can tell the third person and you can "overhear," or they may just feel safer with someone else in the room.

8. *Work with your ex-spouse to establish a supportive framework for making decisions about the children* so that you can present a united front in the future. This minimizes the children's confusion, keeps them from having to choose sides, and prevents them from playing the two of you against one another. The more considerate and cooperative you are with one another, the easier it will be on your children—and on you.

Your children's hangovers are not something about which you can afford to say, "Oh, they'll get over it in time" or "Why focus on it? It'll just make things worse." Their relationships with themselves and their future relationships with others are at stake. The longer your children's hangovers stay in place, the more destructive they become.

Helping your children to heal is actually very simple. If you ever get confused, just remember to tell the truth and make sure they know how much you love them.

Parenting and the Hangover

The first step in parenting effectively after a divorce is to let go of the idea that you did something terrible to your children by ending the marriage.

"WHAT WE DID TO THEM"

Alex has been divorced for three years and is involved with a woman whom he loves deeply, but he has no plans ever to marry again. "I just couldn't take the chance of putting myself or the kids through another divorce," he says. "I felt like I let them down and made it so they won't have good marriages. I really screwed up."

Sherry, 9, and Conal, 11, can use guilt about the divorce to get anything they want from Alex. "I'd have better grades if I had a *real* family," Conal says. Sherry chimes in, "I won't feel *comfortable* if I can't have a new dress for Susie's party. She has a dad *and* a mom." Until Alex handles the "children" part of his own hangover, he won't be able to help them deal with theirs.

THE MYTH OF "STAYING TOGETHER FOR THE CHILDREN"

It is absolutely false that children's best interests are served by parents staying together, no matter what. Guilt over this myth is a waste of time and energy, and may actually compound your children's problems. As the children of parents who *should* have divorced and *didn't* will be the first to tell you, staying together "for the children" can be far more destructive than any divorce.

The myth makes it easier to stay in a relationship that is no longer vital, but there is nothing in it for the children. The impact of divorce, even a traumatic one, is less stressful for them than remaining in a troubled home. Divorce is clear; a troubled home is not. Divorce happens within a finite time; a troubled home does not. It is a destructive environment of confused relationships, anxiety, and fear that can actually make children physically ill. It reinforces negative emotional patterns that can stay in place for the rest of their lives.

If your marriage wasn't working, you did the right thing to get a divorce—for yourself and for your children. Holding on to guilt keeps you stuck in the hangover and may even give them one.

CHILDREN'S SIXTH SENSE

Children know when something is wrong. They have a sixth sense, a heightened awareness about their parents because they once depended on you for survival and may still connect their well-being to yours. If the marriage is in trouble or has broken down completely, *they know it—no matter what you tell them*. It doesn't fool them for a minute when you say, "Mommy and Daddy are just having a discussion. Everything's fine." It only confuses them.

When they can't count on their protectors for the truth, their reality begins to break down and their survival feels threatened. The emotional atmosphere is stiff, tense, and uncertain. No one knows what is really happening, and everyone is walking on eggshells. In this case, divorce is actually a relief not only for the partners, but for the children, as well.

When a marriage is being kept intact "for the children," the messages the children get are:

- It is their fault that everyone is so unhappy.
- Something very important that threatens their survival is being kept hidden; they can't know what it is or do anything about it.
- Authentic emotions are forbidden and must be kept secret.

It is much easier for children to deal with an honest divorce than a faked family.

CHILDREN LEARN BY EXAMPLE

Children learn how to treat themselves and others by watching us. They absorb information from us with staggering speed and accuracy. They will treat themselves the way they see us treating ourselves. They will relate to others the way they see us relating. If we stay in destructive, inauthentic relationships, that is what they will learn to do.

As a child, Perry heard his father ridiculing his mother and watched her retaliate by manipulating him with guilt. Years later, when he sought counseling to deal with the end of his marriage, he realized he had recreated the same dynamic in his relationship.

Of all the gifts you can give your children, respect and appreciation for themselves and others is the best guarantee of their future happiness and success with people.

WHAT IS "RESPONSIBLE PARENTING"?

You have three responsibilities to your children:

1. To provide for their physical and emotional needs: food, clothing, shelter, and love.
2. To teach, by example, healthy ways of relating to themselves and to other people.
3. To help them develop self-reliance and competence in the outside world.

All three of these responsibilities can be met *after* a divorce. Being married is no guarantee against poor parenting and parenting after divorce can be both responsible and effective.

Your children are the fruit of your relationship, and may have been the best part of your marriage. That promise can be fulfilled even if the relationship no longer exists.

4 PARENTING PITFALLS

Parenting after a divorce is much the same as parenting before a divorce, but there are a few special pitfalls:

1. Drawing your children into the battle with your ex-spouse.

One of the easiest ways to attack your ex-spouse is to be sarcastic, demeaning, bitter, victimized, angry, wistful, or critical when talking about him or her to the children. Sometimes the temptation is almost overwhelming. DON'T DO IT.

There is nothing more frightening to children than to see

one of their protectors, their sources of security, being attacked or undermined by the other.

Children need to believe in both of their parents. They see themselves as part of you, and part of your ex-spouse; if one of you is bad, then they feel that they are half-bad. Criticizing your ex-spouse not only maintains your own hangover, it contributes to your children's hangovers. Their loyalties become confused and bad feelings begin to fester.

Betty was so filled with hatred for her ex-husband that she went to court to get her son's name changed so that he wouldn't have the same last name as his father. The child was left with the impression that part of him was so monstrous that he couldn't even use that name.

Regardless of what your ex-spouse has done to *you*, show respect and appreciation for his or her role as your children's other parent. When you treat your ex-spouse with consideration and respect, you both keep your dignity in the children's eyes. They need this in order to feel secure. It's something you have to do for their sakes, whether or not it comes naturally.

If you and your ex-spouse have different approaches to parenting, don't be critical of his or her method. Instead, say something like, "Mommy has her way of doing things, I have my way. That's wonderful because as you grow up, you'll have two ways from which to choose."

If something specific is bothering you about the other person's parenting, or about how the two of you are relating to the children, talk to your ex-spouse about it. It may involve choices about school or vacations, problems the children are having, or individual situations you think the other parent might be able to handle better than you could. Don't present your concerns as threats or challenges to his or her relationship with the children, but as concerns you share because you are on the same team and are both concerned about their well-being.

You don't have to go overboard with the children and heap insincere praise on your ex-spouse, insisting that she is "the greatest mother in the world" if she is not. Your children know the truth about her and will hear the false note in your voice.

Emphasize the positive—"She loves you very much"—but don't ask for trouble by stretching the truth.

Respect your children enough to be honest, and remember that whenever you speak about their other parent, you are talking about part of *them*.

2. Buying children's affection.

This is a temptation whether you are the "weekend" or the "weekday" parent. There is a tendency to try to "make up for what you've done to them" or to raise your own position in their eyes with material possessions, extravagant outings or parties, and generally spending a lot of money to prove that you love them.

It doesn't work—for them or for you. Children respond to love, not to things, no matter how excited they may initially appear about extravagant gifts.

Joanna's parents were divorced when she was nine, and her room looked like her friends' idea of heaven. She had her own computer, phone, answering machine, television, and CD player, in addition to a closet full of designer clothes and pictures of her horse over her desk. Joanna was not a happy child. She rarely saw her father, who paid most of these bills, and her mother was too busy to spend much time with her. By the time she was eleven, she had been caught shoplifting and was constantly in trouble at school.

Some people are overly generous with their children because it infuriates their ex-spouse. A competition develops, pitting the two parents against one another in a battle for the children's attention and affection.

The new stepparent may go overboard in an effort to assuage guilt. My daughter had a little friend who was the "beneficiary" of this situation. One Christmas this child gave her playmates extravagant presents like bikes and small TV's. My daughter was confused and wanted to reciprocate until I pointed out that these were not appropriate presents for children to give one another. Instead, my daughter baked cookies and arranged them in attractive little boxes that she had made herself.

Being overly indulgent with your children is not healthy; it is counterproductive both for them and for you.

3. Confusing hangover symptoms with the normal insanity of growing up.

How can you tell whether your child is exhibiting symptoms of a severe divorce hangover or just growing up, with all the craziness that this process entails?

Like it or not, you are usually dealing with many dramatic changes when your children are between the ages of twelve and twenty. It is often difficult to distinguish between the normal insanity of this time and the symptoms of the divorce hangover. You just have to take your best shot and, when in doubt, *ask your children*.

If they show up for breakfast with spiked-out green hair, refuse to speak anything but German, start dating rap musicians when their only social activity heretofore has been the debate society, or engage in other startling activities and behaviors, you might ask them if something new is going on in their lives, if something is bothering them, and if they want to talk about it.

Don't automatically use the divorce as the scapegoat; their behavior could be entirely normal, or normally abnormal. They may grow out of it in a week if you leave them alone. The one sure way to make the strange behavior stick is to resist it or give them a lot of negative attention for it.

Highly unusual or inappropriate behaviors—dramatic physical differences, wild mood swings, staying out too late or all night, refusing to leave the bedroom, etc.—deserve some attention, but don't approach your children as if they have done something wrong. Especially in early adolescence, when children are becoming more aware of themselves physically, their behaviors are likely to be erratic.

Nicole started having trouble in school soon after her parents' divorce. She found it hard to concentrate, her grades were slipping, and many of her friends dropped her because she was getting so much attention from the boys. Her mother couldn't tell whether Nicole's problems stemmed from the divorce, or from the fact that most of the characters in this drama were fourteen years old. Nicole was in no shape to tell her.

The mother had a choice of how to handle this situation. She chose to treat it as a normal developmental crisis and said, "I remember that this was a very hard time for me, too. You just have to trust that you'll get through it, that everybody's hormones will ultimately settle down, and that you'll meet friends who'll stick by you."

Girls may turn into little Camilles who get sick at the drop of a hat and "*cannot* go to school." You might say, "Do you realize that you have missed ten out of the last thirty school days? You're not sickly, so let's talk about this. What's going on at school? Is something scaring or upsetting you?" The chances are good that it's something to do with her friends, and that you can support her in handling it.

Boys are more likely to act out by throwing themselves around physically, tapping their feet, and seeming to be constitutionally incapable of sitting still. This is normal, but not always appropriate. You might say, "Do you realize that you're having tremendous difficulty sitting still? Is something bothering you, or do you just need to get on your bike and ride as hard and fast as you can? You have all this wonderful energy. Is there some way we can figure out how to use it?"

The solutions are the same whether you are dealing with divorce hangover or everyday craziness. Talk to your children. Find out and accept where they are and what is bothering them. Do what you can to support them in moving through this crisis and on into the next one. Remember that we are not speaking here of *eliminating* crises—they are what growing up is made of—but rather, of moving through them with as much grace and love as possible.

Check in with your children periodically and give them an opportunity to talk about anything that may be bothering them about the divorce or its aftermath, but don't panic or jump to conclusions if they act strangely.

4. Making the divorce an excuse to act out because they are "the poor children."

Anyone who feels sorry for your children because of the divorce shouldn't be around them. Don't let anyone suggest to them that the divorce is a reason to do badly in school or to have behavioral problems. Any kid worth his salt will jump on this information and say, "Ah *ha!* Now I can get away with murder! I can do anything! I'm from a *broken home!*"

The basic message you want to communicate is: "Look, it may be tough sometimes without Dad (or Mom) living here, but together we can help each other handle this. Today is Monday, tomorrow is Tuesday, I love you, and we're going to work through these things together. Dad (or Mom) loves you and life goes on. We're going to see how much fun we can have with these new circumstances."

There is no reason for children not to believe this message *unless someone tells them differently.* Even if they can't talk yet, children know exactly what is happening if someone comes on the scene with a bowed head saying, or even thinking, "Oh, these poor children . . . what a tragedy!" Don't think those sweet children won't use this for all it's worth; they are in survival mode, and they will grab anything they can get their hands on.

I'm in favor of telling teachers, coaches, and other adults who have a lot of contact with the children, what is going on and how you are handling it. They need to know that the children are going through a crisis and may show some subtle changes, but they also need to know what your stance is: This is a tough time, but it shouldn't be used as an excuse. Say to the people in your children's lives, "This is how I'm handling it. If you're not able to do this, please let me know."

The day after we told our six-year-old son that we were getting divorced, he went to school and announced to everyone, "My parents are getting a divorce." I thought this was a healthy reaction. He didn't treat it as something he should be embarrassed about. Instead, he put everyone on notice that something different would be going on in his life.

When Nicole was having trouble with her young friends because of the boys' attention, her mother could have made the mistake of blaming everything on the divorce and said, "Well,

I'm sure that the divorce was hard on you and changed everything, and I know that the way your father's been acting is *very upsetting* to you. Why don't you just stay home from school today and take it easy. I understand. . . ." This is actually what Nicole's mother might wish someone would say to *her*, but it would have taught Nicole that she had an excuse to do anything she wanted.

Give your children the attention and love they need, but don't let them use the divorce as an excuse to fail, act out in harmful ways, or punish you or your ex-spouse.

THE GIFT OF SELF-RELIANCE

Divorce is a chance for children to learn that life contains adversity, but that they can grow and become stronger by facing challenges.

Their natural instincts to grow and become more competent are stifled when they think they can score points with you by acting dependent. If you feel important and needed when they whine, "I can't do this," then they may prefer making you feel better to developing their own strengths.

The message you want to give them is: "Your life is secure not only because I will be here, but because you yourself are competent and know how to take care of your needs. I love you, but I may have to go out and work, or work harder. Look what you get to do, though. You can plan your own menus, learn to take care of your own clothes, and a lot of new, grownup things. You are an essential member of the new team, someone who is strong and able to make a contribution."

No matter how old we are, all of us feel a sense of pride when we learn to do something new and are no longer dependent on someone else for that thing. When children learn to tie their own shoelaces, make their own peanut butter and jelly sandwiches, or pour their own milk, *they have accomplished something* and of course they let you know it.

At seven, my son had to transfer three times to ride the bus downtown to school. His ability to do this made him high as a kite. He was so pleased with himself that he couldn't wait to get home and tell me he'd come up with three different routes he could take. He knew how to get around the city better than I did, and I told him so!

Most of us underestimate children and are surprised when we read in the paper about the strength, ingenuity, and heroism of the five-year-old who drove a car to save her brother's life, or the eight-year-old who lifted a fallen tree off his sister's leg.

We forget that they are capable not only of these physical feats, but also of extraordinary emotional and psychological feats and understanding—even when they don't have the vocabulary to express them.

The two best ways to nurture self-reliance are to remember how competent and resilient children are, and to teach by example—to understand how able and self-reliant you yourself are. Let your children be strong, but don't forget that a hug can feel good at any age.

SINGLE PARENTING

Single parenting after a divorce can be a real adjustment. There is only one of you to do all the things that two people did, you are apt to be more tired, and you may not have as much money. This is a real challenge if the other parent is out of the picture completely.

If you are the "weekend" parent, there will be a temptation to make each moment special by trying to entertain them as a form of compensation. If you see your children even less often, it is virtually impossible to avoid awkwardness until you "settle in" with each other. You, and they, may have to make some adjustments in terms of sleeping arrangements, schedules, and how much of your life and your friends they share. The key is to stay flexible and keep in communication with them.

If you are the "weekday" parent, it's easy to become a martyr. The time they spend with the "weekend" parent is entertaining, recreational time, but *you* are the one who makes sure they do their chores, gets them up to go to school, and generally presides over the "work" part of their lives. When this dynamic emerged in my family, I just mentioned to the children as lightly as I could, "Let's just remember that most of your recreational time is spent with him and your everyday work stuff is with me. That's the way we set it up and the way we want it, but sometimes I miss that easy, relaxed time with you."

As a single parent, you must take care of yourself. That means having a life away from your children. One night out a week is a must, whether or not you think you "should."

Single parenting is simply parenting. You may have to be more patient and call on deeper reserves within yourself, but the principles remain the same—love your children, be honest with them, and support them in becoming loving, able, self-reliant people.

At the same time, don't slip into the "perfect parent" role. Not only is it impossible to be a perfect parent, but trying isn't healthy for you or for your children. Let them see what being human is all about.

HELPING THEM HEALS YOU

Your relationship with your children doesn't change just because you are divorced. You are still their teacher and role model—whether you are the "weekend" or the "weekday" parent.

It isn't always easy or convenient to be patient and loving in the midst of your own pain, but it is part of being a parent—and now you can look at it as part of your divorce hangover therapy.

Jo's daughter, Kirsten, 5, would not talk for six months after the divorce. Jo had to spend a great deal of extra time with her, take her to a special therapist, and put aside her frustration at having to deal with this situation when she herself felt most vulnerable and unable to cope.

In the process, she found reserves of love and understanding she never knew were within her, and developed a special bond with Kirsten that never faded. She became a bigger person than she thought she was, and this helped her heal her own hangover much more quickly and easily.

Putting your attention outside yourself, on the young people you love most, can help you get through your own rough times.

As your children heal, you not only have the joy and satisfaction of watching them lead happier and more productive lives—you find that you are healing yourself.

◆

SUMMARY

• The core emotion of children's hangovers is fear.

• The antidotes are telling your children the truth about what is going on and reassuring them of your love. Children are more resilient and practical than parents give them credit for being.

• Hangovers that children "catch" from a parent reflect that parent's hangover.

• Divorce is not inherently "bad for the children."

• A responsible parent provides for the children's physical and emotional needs, teaches by example healthy ways of relating to oneself and others, and helps children develop self-reliance and confidence.

• A responsible parent does not: use the children, buy their affection, confuse normal growing-up insanity with hangover symptoms, let divorce become an excuse for unacceptable behavior.

◆

◆
WORKBOOK EXERCISES
◆

1. Check the guidelines for working with your children during the divorce and write down the ones you may have missed. Go over these with your children.

2. What signals have your children given that indicate hangovers? Verbal signals? Body language? Behavior patterns? Give specific examples.

3. Look at your own hangover behavior and attitudes. Write down ways you will avoid involving your children.

4. Describe how you have covered the three major responsibilities of parenting.

5. Where have you gone overboard? Where do you have more work to do?

6. Give examples of how you have slipped into the 4 parenting pitfalls.

7

◇

Finances

◇

◇

The Secret of a Great Financial Settlement

Finances rival children as the area of greatest conflict in divorce, resulting in divorce hangovers.

The financial settlement is a powerful symbol in our society. It is the most concrete, tangible result of a divorce, the thing that many people hold up to show whether they "won" or "lost," and whether their divorce was a success or a failure.

This attitude is one of the biggest obstacles to getting a fair settlement or healing a divorce hangover.

I want to emphasize here that I am talking about financial settlement, that is, the distribution of the material aspects of the marriage. I am *not* talking about child support, which is the responsibility of *all* parents, especially when one parent is on shaky ground financially. When a divorce is approached with the best interests of the children in mind, the child support issue is not as great. The sad fact of nonpayment of child support is well documented, but there is legal recourse one can seek.

WHY MONEY MAKES US CRAZY

In our society, we have money and possessions all mixed up with our sense of who we are, our creativity, our power, and our survival. It's no wonder we get so voracious when we start cutting up the financial pie and hold so tenaciously to the material aspects of marriage.

It often seems easier to let go of the person we once loved than to let go of the possessions we accumulated with that person. By some act of our own—whether through marriage or through our own earning power—we brought those things into our lives. We are identified with them and guard them jealously. Often, they have more meaning to us than their actual monetary value.

Ben didn't mind dividing up most of their property, but he absolutely refused to give Rena shares in the company he had founded. That was his territory, and he didn't want her to have anything to do with it.

Ronnie insisted on getting three quarters, rather than half, of the money from the sale of the home she had decorated. She wanted to be compensated not only for increasing the house's value, but also for the anguish she suffered for having to leave it.

Money and things are tangible and definable. They lend themselves to balance sheets and market values. They become convenient yardsticks against which to measure our self-worth, however misleading and destructive that measurement may be. They are the chips we use to keep score of how we're doing in the divorce. We count how much is in our pot and how much is in the other person's pot, and then try to get more of everything into ours.

Lee tried to get back the self-esteem she lost when Gordon left her for a younger woman by filling her pot with nearly everything the two of them had owned. He left the marriage with little more than the shirt on his back.

Drew said, "I lost her; I'll be damned if I'll lose the divorce, too!" He hired expensive lawyers and cut Jessica out of almost everything in an effort to "balance things out."

Neither Lee nor Drew felt as good as they'd expected to after taking their ex-spouses to the cleaners. In fact, they felt even worse.

SURVIVAL!

All of the things we associate with finances are threatened in the vulnerable time around a divorce—control, identity, creativity, and self-worth—but there is an even deeper, more primitive reason that we cling so desperately to material things. We associate them with our very survival—with the raw, basic needs for food, clothing, and shelter. On some subliminal level, perhaps we feel we can never get enough of those things to feel truly safe.

This is not to *excuse* greed, but rather to *understand* that all of us have these kinds of instincts. It helps to remember that we are all human. But it is also true that human beings feel better about themselves when they rise above those baser instincts into a spirit of forgiveness, cooperation, and generosity.

THE SIZE OF THE PIE

Divorce is never the windfall that some people expect it to be. If the financial picture the couple shared amounts to one pie, it doesn't make sense to imagine that one person would walk away from the divorce with two pies.

The pie is the same size as it always was. When it is divided between two people, no matter who gets the bigger piece, both people have smaller portions than they had when they were sharing the whole pie. Male or female, and regardless of who made more money, you both have less after a divorce than you did before.

For some reason, Tracy had expected her divorce to be a cornucopia. She had heard stories of women becoming fabulously wealthy after their divorces and had naively believed them.

Before her divorce, Tracy lived with her husband and two children in the Chicago townhouse which they owned. The children had gone to private schools and she did freelance public relations. After the divorce, she lived in the same townhouse, the children went to the same schools, and she still did public relations—except that now she had to take some jobs that she wouldn't have taken before the divorce, when they didn't really need her income to make the household run smoothly.

Tracy felt she had been beaten up in the financial settlement, even though she got the townhouse and most of its contents, some transition alimony, and generous child support. She complained about her ex-husband, Dwight, about having to work harder, and about the unfairness of it all. In actuality, Dwight's standard of living had been affected far more than hers. He was in a small apartment in a less desirable neighborhood, and struggling to maintain some semblance of his former lifestyle while virtually supporting hers.

It wasn't until they both sat down with a reputable financial advisor and started putting everything down on paper that Tracy realized her settlement was more than equitable. It just felt difficult because she had most of the same expenses, but not as much money.

Diminished circumstances may not be comfortable, but most people can deal with them once they accept reality. The problem arises when you expect a windfall and actually wind up with less.

MYTH: THE *SIZE* OF THE SETTLEMENT DETERMINES THE SUCCESS OF THE DIVORCE

This myth is as untrue and as harmful as the myth that you should stay together for the sake of the children.

The success of your divorce has nothing to do with the size of the settlement. These are some things a good financial settlement is *not*:

1. *A good financial settlement is* not *one in which you make out like a bandit*; it is one in which your financial

unit is divided into two separate parts and each party has an economic base from which to enter the next phase of his or her life. It is one in which you separate your lives physically, emotionally, and financially, and move forward into the future without resentment or bad feelings.

2. *A good financial settlement is* not *determined by how much you get, but by how you feel about yourself, your ex-spouse, and the divorce.* No amount of money is worth your peace of mind, well-being, or self-esteem. If either party feels exploited, the two of you are still bound together in a struggle, postponing once more the day when you end your old life and begin a new one.

3. *A good financial settlement is* not *one which determines who is right or wrong.* There should be no moral judgment, no hint of reward or punishment in the settlement. Once you start dealing in right and wrong, reward and punishment, these judgments pervade all the other areas of your divorce. Blame and guilt are back in the equation—and you cannot resolve a divorce hangover when they are present.

4. *A good financial settlement is* not *an emotional weapon,* a way to beat up your ex-spouse or continue the destructive drama of the divorce. Emotional needs cannot be fulfilled with numbers and balance sheets. Acting out anger, hurt, vindictiveness, or victimhood in the financial settlement never works.

WHAT IS A SUCCESSFUL SETTLEMENT?

The success of a financial settlement is determined by two criteria:

- Did you separate the economic entity into two parts?
- Did you both come away feeling good about yourselves and financially equipped to start the next phase of your lives?

A good financial settlement should be two things:

1. *Transitional.* It is a vehicle for moving out of the old financial relationship and into a new phase of financial independence.
2. *Firm.* Once both parties have agreed to it, it should be a closed issue. Being able to go back and renegotiate each week doesn't serve anybody.

Working out a financial settlement that is acceptable to both parties is the cornerstone of a successful divorce. Without it, you will always hear footsteps—either yours or the other person's. If this issue is not resolved, it becomes the perfect vehicle for a divorce hangover.

I know one couple who have been "divorced" for almost ten years but have yet to resolve their financial settlement. They are deeply embroiled in their hangovers, with no prospect of recovery until they work out the money and property.

17 GUIDELINES FOR WORKING OUT A FINANCIAL SETTLEMENT

If you are in the midst of a divorce now, use these guidelines to avoid a financial hangover. If you are healing a hangover, let them help pinpoint the roots of your anger or resentment.

These guidelines are based on a spirit of cooperation and generosity. Ideally, both people will abide by these principles. But one person using them is better than none, and you may find that your partner becomes more generous in the process.

As with all aspects of divorce, anything that minimizes future backlash from your ex-spouse is in your best interest and frees you to move forward.

General Principles

1. *Avoid communicating through lawyers.* The two of you are one another's best source of information; any strategies you develop will work better if you are both

behind them. Messages that have to pass through several people are often distorted; the fewer "middle men," the better. Although most lawyers have high professional ethics, keep in mind that it is in their financial interest for your divorce and financial settlement to be both difficult and prolonged. (See Chapter 8 for dealing with lawyers.)

2. *Remember that the pie is the same size as it was before the divorce.* Don't expect to get $100,000 if you only had $50,000 in the bank.

3. *See a financial advisor* to get an accurate picture of each person's needs. You will need to do your homework and spend some time developing budgets before you do this. If the woman has not been self-supporting, for instance, or if her income isn't enough to support herself and the children, then she may need some help during this transition period. It may be in everyone's best interest for her to get the extra training or education she needs to increase her earning power and become independent.

   A financial advisor can help you set up structures that take the guesswork and uncertainty out of this process. These structures give the woman certainty that her needs will be met, and give the man certainty about exactly what his obligations will be. He is less likely to be taken back to court later because the woman knows what she can realistically expect and what she can't.

4. *Complete the financial arrangement as soon as possible.* In many states, the divorce settlement and the financial settlement are completed separately, and the financial settlement can drag on and on. Don't let this happen. The sooner everything is final, the sooner the wounds start to heal.

Possessions

5. *Divide your possessions into categories* (furniture, china, electronic equipment, etc.) and try not to split them up so that, for instance, you each wind up with five plates but no one has the whole set of ten.

6. *Set aside items that are more precious to one of you than the other.* Items with special emotional value are in an entirely different category. Their monetary value may not come into play at all, and you can negotiate about them later.

7. *Also set aside items that were purchased for one person's use (a car, for example).* You can negotiate about these later, too.

8. *When you have two of one item (televisions, for example), don't haggle about who gets which one or which one is more valuable.* It's not worth it.

9. *Let the places to which you are moving solve problems whenever possible.* If one new place has carpeting, for instance, the other person gets the old rugs.

10. *If neither of you wants certain possessions, sell them and divide the profits.*

11. *Each of you should be able to keep items that belonged to your family.*

12. *If both of you want a certain item,* try to make an even trade by finding something, or several things, equally prized by the other person. If you can't find an equitable trade, flip a coin (after agreeing to abide by the outcome!).

Money, Income, and Equity

13. *If both of you are self-supporting,* simply divide up the savings, securities, equity, etc. You are the lucky ones.

14. *If one of you is the established "breadwinner,"* set up a structure to support the other, with the condition that the other person get on his or her feet financially as

soon as possible. This fund may include money for more training or education.

15. *Establish a specific plan, and a schedule, for the other person to become independent.* This benefits both people. No one wants to be an albatross around someone else's neck indefinitely. If there is financial dependency, the relationship is still unresolved.

16. *Child support should be considered* aside from *the financial settlement between the husband and wife.* One should have no bearing on the other; they are two entirely separate issues.

17. *Beware of the jungle.* Watch out for the grasping, survival-oriented jungle mentality that surfaces around money and possessions. Not only will it wreak havoc with the quality of your life, but the energy behind it will not attract all those wonderful things—or a mate—back into your life.

You do not have to go after your ex-spouse tooth and nail in order to survive. You are going to be fine, even if you have to rely entirely on your own wits. You gathered all those things around you once; you can do it again! Relax and trust your ability to make things happen.

Your energy, time, and spirit are your greatest assets. Don't throw them away in a pointless battle against your ex-spouse, or waste them on fear or worry.

Hangover Finances

As I said earlier, bad feelings about the financial settlement can be one of the fiercest parts of the hangover. Fortunately, there is a simple, instantaneous, foolproof method for healing them.

MEN, WOMEN, MONEY, AND NO-FAULT DIVORCE

Most young women today reject the model of men as breadwinners and women as homemakers with no access to money except through their husbands. Yet this attitude still holds sway with both men and women in much of our culture— whether or not we admit it.

Women who have depended on men for financial support are often eager to perpetuate this system, believing that they are better off trying to find a man who will do well than trying to do well themselves.

Those who believe that no-fault divorce is harmful to women have adopted this premise. Their grievance is that when there is no fault to be found, then there is no punishment reflected in the financial settlement and women generally come away with less money. It is true that since such women usually have less initial earning power as well, their circumstances are often reduced quite dramatically, but this premise keeps women stuck in the role of victims who can't take care of themselves or their children. It suggests that women must always look outside themselves—to a man or to the courts—to achieve what they want in life. I believe that if women look instead for ways to succeed, they will.

Everyone who knew Ginny agreed that no-fault divorce had done her in. Even though he was paying child support, Cliff had enough money and earning power that his lifestyle changed only slightly. Six months later, he was vacationing in the south of France with his new girlfriend. Ginny, on the other hand, was struggling to pay rent and buy food for herself and their two boys, ages five and seven.

She had spent a good part of that six months blaming Cliff and the courts for her situation and plotting how to get back at him. Finally she realized that this had been a complete waste of her time and energy. She gradually began to accept what she had suspected all along, that no one was going to rescue her. Unless she did something herself, she and the boys would spend at least the next fifteen years in poverty.

She sat down with a close friend one Saturday afternoon and worked out a plan. Ginny's most obvious asset was that she was a fantastic cook and loved to entertain. She borrowed $2000 from her mother to tide her over and started a catering business. For the first few weeks, she took samples of her gourmet entrees and desserts around to local businesses and associations that used caterers. One client signed up, then another. In three months, she was breaking even, and within a year she had a full-time staff of four.

Ginny rose to the challenge and made a whole new life for herself once she gave up blame and self-pity. Instead of continuing to see herself as a victim of no-fault divorce, she made it work in her favor.

Sinking back into the realm of blame and fault-finding keeps everyone stuck. It is far more detrimental to women than being offered a challenge.

GROUND-BREAKING ATTITUDES

Both men and women have to adopt radical new attitudes in order to heal financial hangovers. Vince and Dee's situation illustrates what doesn't work about our present attitudes.

Vince paid very generous alimony and child support to Dee and their three children, and never seemed to mind until he married Charlotte. After the birth of their first child, Vince's visits to his three other children became much less frequent. He notified Dee that he could no longer afford to send any alimony and that he would be reducing the child support payments.

She became hysterical. "I gave up my career and my life for you! I don't know how to make a living! I've been stuck at home with the kids for ten years. We'll starve to death!" she screamed.

"Yeah, *ten years!*" he yelled back. "You're the only woman I know who doesn't work. What am I, a money machine?! Get a job! Get a life!"

Women have to let go of the idea that they are inept or less able than men are to take care of themselves. They have to grasp the situation as an opportunity to find new strengths and abilities.

This represents an enormous change, a fundamental shift in the way men and women relate, and in the way women perceive themselves. I'm not saying it is an easy shift, or that everyone can make it overnight, or that you won't meet with some resistance. I am saying that it is the only way out of the cycle of dependency and helplessness, and the only way to be able to say, "I did it *myself*."

It is a step you have to take to be free of the hangover. If you are still dependent on your ex-spouse in any way (aside from transitional and child support), the hangover cannot be fully healed.

Men also need to adopt some new attitudes. Some "enlightened" men pay lip service to no-fault divorce as an expression of equality between the sexes, but in fact, they like it because it's apt to be less expensive for them. Some take a secret delight in watching their ex-wives squirm financially and can't imagine that "the little woman" could actually take care of herself.

These men need to develop a more genuine support for women discovering their power and talents, and to understand that their ex-wives may need some tangible, monetary support at first to achieve those ends.

Some men play an active role in their children's lives after a divorce, both emotionally and financially, but others are inclined to withdraw their money as well as their energy from the marriage and anything that reminds them of it, including their children. They feel burdened and resentful about alimony or child support, especially if they have started a new relationship or family, and either disappear from the old situation entirely or withhold energy from it, putting all their resources into the new relationship and the children of that marriage.

To heal their financial hangovers, men need to recognize and accept at least partial monetary responsibility for *all* of their children. They have to stop thinking of this obligation as a terrible burden, and remember that those children are still part of them regardless of what happened with the children's mother.

THE WAR OF THE ROSES

When couples give in to their worst instincts, financial hangovers can degenerate into a brutal battle of wills.

The words may be very civil and polite, and all the communication may slip smoothly through lawyers in Italian suits, but just beneath the surface, the man is screaming, "*I've got it all and you don't, and you aren't going to get anything except the crumbs I want to toss you!*" The woman is screaming back, "*You're going to be sorry you were ever born and ever looked at another woman. I'm not going to accept anything less than everything!*"

In the film *The War of the Roses*, Michael Douglas and Kathleen Turner fought this battle literally to the death. Their nightmarish portrayal of a couple who get caught in the lowest level of physical and emotional survival should be required viewing for everyone involved in a divorce or divorce hangover.

One couple I know acted out their struggle in a War of the Monkey Teapot. Meg had become involved with another man and Gene was very bitter. She got some alimony and almost unlimited child support, but very few possessions. He kept the house, but she was allowed to come in and take some things that had belonged to her family. While she was there, she picked up a monkey teapot of which she was very fond and started to put it with her other things.

"You can't have that," Gene shouted. "It's in the house and it's mine!"

She insisted that she had a right to it, that she had used it every day and was attached to it. Gene tried to take it away from her and, in the scuffle, the monkey teapot crashed to the floor and shattered into a million pieces.

As always in these kinds of battles, nobody won.

A RADICAL SOLUTION TO THE SETTLEMENT BLUES

The bottom line in healing the financial part of your hang-over, whether you are a man or a woman, is to *accept as reality the financial settlement that you have now and put everything else behind you.*

Again, I'm not talking about child support here. I know some women who in the confusion of the divorce did not negotiate enough child support from husbands who *were* able to pay more. These women opted to go back to court.

Accepting your reality means no more second-guessing yourself or your ex-spouse about whether or not you got a good deal; no more anger, resentment, or gnashing of teeth about *not* getting a good deal; no more guilt about having gotten a terrific deal.

What you have now is all there is. Equitable or not, that is your only reality.

You should contact your ex-spouse and go back to court *only if you feel you received* too much *of the pie.* If you want to give some of it back, pick up the phone and make him or her an offer.

If you feel that you got cheated, however, don't sit by the phone waiting for your ex-spouse to call. *Accept what you have now, give up resentments and regrets, and move forward with your life.* The time for wish lists is over. You can't reach back into the past and do things differently. Hoarding bad feelings about the settlement costs you your peace of mind and changes nothing.

I'm not talking about giving up or rolling over and playing dead. I am talking about making a conscious decision for your own sake to release all the anxiety, anger, and turmoil around the financial part of your divorce. This is an investment in yourself, in your future, and in the quality of your life.

Financial Independence

The process of becoming financially independent is a tremendous opportunity to build self-esteem, whether you are a man or a woman. It is also an essential part of healing a divorce hangover. Financial independence changes everything for the better, even if you're starting from the bottom and working toward something more in keeping with your expectations and ambitions. You no longer have to look to your ex-spouse, or to the financial settlement, to rescue you. This gives you a tremendous freedom that is very difficult to achieve if you need your ex-spouse's goodwill or legal obligation in order to pay the rent.

This section is directed mainly to women who have not been the breadwinner during marriage and feel frightened when they look up and discover that they are now on their own.

MAKING THE BREAK

Cutting the economic ties can be uncomfortable, especially if you have never been on your own or if you have not worked for many years.

Some people have the luxury of a transition period in which they can get some training or education, but others have to begin supporting themselves *immediately* either for psychological reasons or because the ex-spouse is no longer able or willing to provide support. Whether you are reading this a few months or several years after your divorce, you may need—or want—to get out there *now* and do something.

Esther and her eight-year-old daughter were completely dependent on Reid even though the marriage had ended three years earlier. He lorded it over them, showing up without notice and expecting her to cook and occasionally to have sex. She felt she couldn't refuse him anything; at the slightest hint of rebellion, he would threaten to withhold the checks.

After one such humiliating experience, Esther decided she had to put a stop to the situation immediately. She returned Reid's checks and wouldn't let him in the house. This was a healthy decision, but she had not worked since they were married and had to find ways to stay afloat until she could get her financial feet on the ground.

She began by selling cosmetics at a downtown department store. This was barely enough to support herself and her daughter, but they made it through the first difficult year and Esther was exhilarated by her success. She wasn't making much money, but she felt terrific about herself and was having a great time discovering new talents and making new friends. Financial success followed when she became a buyer and later a sales representative for one of the large cosmetics companies.

She would never have found this new life, or her new sense

of self, if she had stayed under Reid's thumb or had not been willing to start at the bottom and work up.

STAYING AFLOAT IN THE SHORT TERM

Never be afraid to take a low-paying or unskilled job for the short term while you continue to look for what you really want. In my work as a career counselor, I hear people say all the time, "But I don't want to do that." You may not want that particular job at this particular time, but if the rent is due, you may have to take it temporarily.

Very few people can walk directly into the job of their dreams, but don't let that stop you from doing *something*. Do whatever you have to do to support yourself while you make plans for a more gracious future.

YOU ARE YOUR OWN BEST ASSET

Be creative during this time. Everybody has some talent or skill, whether or not it is the result of training or education. Many women have recognized their "cottage industry" skills only after they were forced to earn a living, and then parlayed them into fortunes. Such abilities as baking pastries, creating dolls, stitchery, quilting, and interior design might have gone unnoticed and unappreciated if these talented women hadn't *needed* to make them available to the rest of the world.

Don't underestimate yourself. You probably have skills that you've taken for granted all these years. It's time to place some value on them, and on yourself, and put them to work for you. Devote some time and energy to looking at what those skills and talents might be.

LIVING GRACEFULLY IN THE LONG TERM

You don't need a mansion to live gracefully; all you need are self-reliance, confidence in your ability to make your own way in life, and peace with yourself and your past. Self-esteem isn't measured by the amount of your income, but by how you feel about yourself—and a part of this involves your work.

Start plotting your own course and arranging your own destiny. Not everyone can expect to be like Mrs. Fields, who turned her cookies into an empire, but it is inspiring to learn and think about other women's successes. Get together with like-minded friends, research some of these stories, and support one another as a group.

When you heal the parts of your hangover that involve children and finances, you have it made. The rest begins to fall like a house of cards. Letting go of past dependencies acts like a shot in the arm; you make an enormous commitment to yourself that yields rich rewards.

SUMMARY

- The size of the financial settlement does not dictate the success or failure of the divorce.

- The secret of a successful financial settlement is to recognize that it is simply an economic solution that equitably divides one entity into two, offers the best financial package for both parties, and gives each an independent stake in the future.

- Accepting the financial settlement as it stands now eliminates the possibility of property or finances becoming a hangover issue.

- You are your own best asset.

- Financial independence is a cornerstone of self-esteem.

◆

WORKBOOK EXERCISES

◆

1. How have you or your ex-spouse failed to accept the financial settlement? *Pinpoint unresolved bad feelings or emotionally charged issues around your financial settlement.* Write these down.

2. Have your answers to #1 prolonged the connection between you or caused conflicts? Be specific.

3. What skills have you developed running a household and raising a family? List your interests and hobbies.

4. List your financial assets: savings, salable items, investments, property, the financial settlement, etc.

5. List your living costs: car, housing, clothing, utilities, food, taxes, recreation, etc.

6. Depending on the relationship between #4 and #5, where can you cut costs?

7. What salary range is necessary to live reasonably for now?

8. List ways to get the word out that you need a job.

∙ 8 ∙

The Lawyers

◇

We read the world wrong and say that it
deceives us.

—TAGORE
"STRAY BIRDS"

◇

The legal process of divorce can either add another layer to your
hangover, or help you move quickly and smoothly toward reso-
lution. Before hiring a lawyer, it is essential to consider your
motives.

No More Assassins

In our society, we often use lawyers as "hit men" (or
women) who do our legal dirty work for us. Whether we are
involved in a takeover bid, buying a house, or a divorce, they are
the people on the front lines fighting our battles in the courts.
It's tempting to think that *we* aren't doing all those nasty things;
they are.

Lenore fantasized about getting a gun and shooting Mac
after he announced he wanted a divorce in order to marry an
aerobics instructor at his health club. She did the next best thing

and went after him with a lawyer whom her tennis partner, Hazel, had described as "bloodthirsty." She sat down with this lawyer and said, "I want you to kill him off. Wring his neck financially and make him beg for two weekends a year with the kids. I don't care what you have to do; I don't even want to know. I want him punished!"

The lawyer became Lenore's assassin. He dragged the relationship with the aerobics instructor through the local papers, showed staggering damages to Lenore and the kids, almost got Mac banished from the home entirely, and won a financial settlement that set Lenore up for life and made it virtually impossible for Mac ever to get back on his feet.

Mac was ruined financially and emotionally, but Lenore felt almost no responsibility. Hearing of Mac's latest troubles from a mutual friend years later, she shook her head and said, "That lawyer was just brutal. What a vicious little man!"

We use lawyers as weapons in our legal battles and want them to carry our emotional baggage, but it just doesn't work that way. Sooner or later, our actions come back to haunt us.

As Lenore's children grew into adults, it became clear to them what had happened. Although they still weren't crazy about the idea of their father running out on them, they found it hard to forgive their mother for her cruelty. Whatever he had done, this man was still their father and had kept in as much contact as the courts would allow. Their relationship with Lenore was never as warm or trusting as it had been before she had him "done in."

Who's the Boss?

It's easy to believe that we have no control over what happens once the divorce goes to court. The *lawyers* advised us to go for the jugular; we never would have done it on our own. They told us they'd gotten a great deal for another client in exactly this situation. What did we know? They were the experts. By the same token, many lawyers will say they were just doing what the client wanted, so nobody takes responsibility for what happened.

Lawyers are supposed to guide you through the legal process in a methodical, logical, and thorough fashion. It is their job to lay out your options; it is your job to direct them and to make sure they carry out your orders. They work for you; if they aren't doing what you want, you not only *can* fire them, you *must. You are 100 percent responsible for everything the lawyers do.*

Don't be intimidated by their "expertise." If your lawyer suggests something that is obviously not in the spirit of generosity and is going to prolong or intensify your hangover—or your spouse's—don't acquiesce, even with your silence.

Whodunit?

When lawyers are around, there is always a *we* and a *they.* Their presence often breeds adversity and polarization; everybody takes sides and dives into a bunker. It's not that lawyers are difficult or mean-spirited people; it's that they work in an adversarial system and are trained to win. Unless you stop them or redirect them, this is the approach they usually take.

Sometimes you have to control your lawyers' natural instincts for a good fight. My ex-husband and I decided between ourselves what we wanted in the divorce and called a friend who was a lawyer to draw up a legal document reflecting what we'd worked out. He said he could represent only one of us and recommended another attorney to represent me.

After about a week, it became clear that my new lawyer and I were not on the same wavelength. He pounced on me with, "Well, of course you'll get the house, and you'll get custody of the children, and you'll get . . ."

"Wait a minute!" I said. "That isn't what we worked out at all and it isn't what I told you."

"But it's what you can *get!*" he countered. "You don't understand your *rights!*"

"I do understand my rights, I just don't want to turn this

into a punishing experience for my ex-husband. *If you don't understand that, I'm going to have to change lawyers."*

He understood immediately. From that moment on, we moved smoothly toward an amicable solution. The only time my ex-husband and I had any trouble was when we didn't talk to one another, but let our lawyers interpret and negotiate *for* us.

How to Manage Your Lawyer: 4 Strategies

These four strategies will help keep you on track in your dealing with lawyers:

1. *Know what you want before you go in.* Put a plan together before you approach them. Be particularly clear what you want to do about the children and finances.

   This way, you make decisions based on your own feelings and principles. When these choices are left to the lawyers, they often go for as much as the law will allow. You will keep in mind what these decisions mean in terms of your hangover and your own psychological well-being; they will not.

2. *Remember that you are the employer and the lawyers are your employees.* They work for you. You call the shots. Don't be cajoled or bullied into escalating the battle, and don't make them your scapegoats if the blood starts to flow. Manage them; don't let them manage you.

3. *Stay informed.* After you have told the lawyers what you want, find out exactly what they plan to do to carry out the spirit and the letter of your instructions. You are responsible for knowing what they are going to do, and for making sure it is what you want. Don't give your power over to them or let them push you aside because "you don't understand the law."

4. *Caveat emptor. Buyer beware.* Most lawyers understand that their reputation is their most valuable asset,

but remember that both your attorney and your ex-spouse's attorney have everything to gain and nothing to lose by making the divorce and settlement as extended and difficult as possible. This is how they make their living. They aren't going to turn you down if you want to take your ex-spouse back to court every six months. Don't let them make these kinds of decisions for you.

Mediation

Mediation has come into its own recently as a less expensive and less adversarial way to decide legal matters.

A psychologist, clergyman, lawyer, or other trained individual acts as a third party who hears what each person's needs are, gets the two people talking to one another rather than through their lawyers, and helps them work out an agreement acceptable to both of them. The three of you sit down together to work through each issue and, once an agreement is reached, a contract is drawn up to reflect what you have worked out.

The mediator represents *both* people, so it is more difficult for the situation to become adversarial. Since everyone is on the same team working toward a common goal—the agreement—this system is less emotionally draining than fighting it out in court, where everybody except the lawyers stands to lose time, energy, money, and goodwill.

There are no winners or losers in mediation; everybody wins when an agreement is reached. The mediator has no ax to grind. Tempers are less likely to flare because no one is egging you on. The mediator is looking to see where the balance lies, and will work toward something that benefits both of you.

A word of warning: Don't use friends as mediators. This is a very difficult and tricky role and requires special training. Even professional mediators rarely perform this service for their friends.

Mediation isn't for everybody, but it is a good way to avoid adding to or deepening a hangover.

The Legal Hangover

The laws in many states allow you to do almost anything you want about the financial settlement, custody, and visitation rights—during or after the divorce. You can decide you didn't get enough and take your ex-spouse back to court as many times as you want. This is valuable for some people, but for others, it feeds the divorce hangover.

IF YOU GO AFTER YOUR EX-SPOUSE

What if you are miserable with your financial settlement or the visitation situation? Should you go back to court and try to change it?

We have said that the best solution is to work with what you have and rise to whatever challenges that situation presents. This applies not just to finances but to custody, visitation, and all other issues.

If your settlement was truly terrible, you may have to take one day a month to cry, scream, feel sorry for yourself, and be utterly miserable about it. But spend the other twenty-nine days doing something more productive.

If you take your ex-spouse back to court, remember:

1. *You will probably get a violent reaction.* Your ex-spouse will probably feel attacked and fight back with every resource at his or her disposal. You will be thrown back into the heat of battle instead of creating solutions. In other words, you are asking for big, big trouble.
2. *You are taking a deliberate step backward into the past, and consciously aggravating your hangover.* This will strengthen the hangover and make it much more difficult for you to let go later. You are trying to repaint a picture that is already finished and hung.
3. *You open up an enormous can of worms.* When you go back to court, they don't look just at the one item that you want changed. Every aspect of the case is reopened

and put back on the table for negotiation. You can actually come away with less than you had when you went in. You, and perhaps your children, are back under the microscope and have to rehash all the painful old material. Your lawyer has to rework your case and this can be enormously expensive. The opposing lawyer can also bring up things that have happened since the original settlement, things you may not wish to discuss. Monica went back to court for more money, but Chad's lawyer concentrated on her recent affair with a young male dancer. She didn't get the money, and almost lost her children.

Some part of the settlement may be important enough that you are willing to go through this scrutiny, but be sure to ask yourself these questions:

- Have I tried to work out a solution with my ex privately?
- How much do I want the change?
- How much am I willing to pay for it?

Only you can determine whether an issue is worth the time, expense, risk, energy, and emotional wear and tear of going back to court—or whether you would be better off applying those assets to your future.

IF YOUR EX-SPOUSE COMES AFTER YOU

These same principles apply if your ex-spouse comes after you. If he or she wants more money, more access to the children, or some other change in the settlement, then you have a choice:

1. *You can give in to knee-jerk anger and fight back with everything you have.* Tell your lawyer to pull out all the stops, and make the other person suffer for rocking the boat.

or

2. *You can reassess the situation reasonably and approach it in the spirit of generosity without becoming a door-mat.* Take an honest, rational look at the other person's demands now that the emotionalism of the original court battle is over. Maybe the agreement *should* be reworked. Maybe it wasn't really equitable, or perhaps conditions have changed and you are comfortable with making some adjustments.

Try to resolve the issues once and for all. If you provide college tuition, will your ex-wife then become financially independent? If you let the children spend every other Christmas with your ex-husband, will he stop pestering you from Thanksgiving on each year?

Even if the other person is clearly taking you back to court just to make your life miserable, *don't get hooked into his or her hangover.* The situation will only degenerate into a pitched battle if you give in to your emotions and throw yourself into the fray. If the other person keeps dragging you back to court with unreasonable demands, follow these guidelines:

1. *Keep your objectivity.* The other person wants to upset you; stay detached and keep your emotional balance. You can't abdicate responsibility completely and say to your lawyers, "Do whatever you see fit but leave me out of it," but neither can you afford to fly off the handle.
2. *Remember that your priority is your own emotional well-being and putting an end to the hangover.* Don't give in on issues that are important to you, but stay open to considering the other person's demands.
3. *Direct your lawyers.* Tell them exactly where you are willing to make adjustments, and where you are not. Be sure that they are aware of your guiding principle of emotional well-being and ending the hangover, and that they don't do anything to jeopardize that. Tell them to

go about their business quickly and efficiently, but without rancor. You don't want to aggravate the situation, only to finish and heal it.

IF CIRCUMSTANCES CHANGE

Sometimes circumstances change so dramatically that new arrangements have to be made.

Five years after Martin and Renee were divorced, their son, Arthur, developed leukemia. He was hospitalized frequently for expensive operations and treatments, and needed full-time care at home. Renee would either have to quit her job and stay home with him, or hire a nurse. She knew she couldn't manage alone.

In the first panicky hours, she envisioned taking Martin back to court and forcing him to help. Their divorce had been rather bitter, and a part of her wanted to say, "You're not going to get near this child, but you're going to pay for everything." When she calmed down, she realized that Martin would *want* to help and that it wouldn't do anyone—least of all Arthur—any good to continue the animosity. She and Martin got together to talk about the situation and decide what financial adjustments they would have to make.

They estimated what expenses they could expect from doctors, the hospital, and home care, and came up with a formula for dealing with these as they arose. Martin agreed to support their household so that Renee could stay home and care for Arthur. Working together to support Arthur actually began to heal their relationship.

In some cases of children who develop chronic, life-threatening illnesses, custody changes if one parent can be more available than the other or if one home can better accommodate the equipment the child needs.

Another major change might be that the person providing child support, or perhaps alimony, is no longer able to work—or that the person receiving alimony wins $5 million in the lottery.

You will know instinctively when the settlement needs to be

adjusted. If you can make those adjustments without going back to court or becoming adversaries, you will be better off. Write down the terms you agree on, but stay flexible in case further changes occur. If Arthur goes into long-term or permanent remission, for example, Renee and Martin will want to alter their agreement again. If he gets worse, they will both have to make further adjustments.

The most important element here is trust between the two ex-partners. In these kinds of extreme cases, you need to be able to count on that support, and no legal document is as reliable as mutual goodwill.

LOOSE ENDS

In most divorces, emotional loose ends stemming from the legal battle contribute to the hangover. Two common ones are:

1. *You feel guilty about the way you treated the other person, or how the lawyer treated that person, during the divorce.* Perhaps the way you acted, or the way you used the legal system, didn't reflect the kind of person you like to think you are.

   If silently forgiving yourself isn't enough, you may want to sit down with the other person and say something like, "It's been awhile since the divorce now and I've come to recognize that I didn't act very well during that time. I feel badly about that and just wanted to say that I'm sorry."

   If you do this, be prepared for the other person to go berserk and attack you verbally if he or she is still under the influence of a hangover. Your words may be interpreted as, "I just want you to know that I *got* you and you lost."

   On the other hand, the other person may be completely disarmed by your willingness to say something conciliatory or nice. It may open up a whole new era in your relationship.

2. *You feel the lawyers took you for a ride,* doing more work than needed to be done, drawing out the process, and overcharging you. This may be true but, as with the settlement, it is better to accept reality as it is and go on from there.

You can sit around gnashing your teeth and sticking pins in a little lawyer doll, or you can get on with life. Use your unlimited legal options to heal, rather than to intensify or expand, your hangover.

For information on fee structures, how to select an attorney, referrals, and other technical matters, call your state bar association.

SUMMARY

- You are the boss; the lawyer works for you, and you are responsible for his or her actions.

- No contract or divorce settlement is irrevocable.

- Using the legal system to go after your ex-spouse just prolongs the hangover. Only your own two feet can carry you backward.

- Remember that your priority is to heal, not to win.

◆

WORKBOOK EXERCISES

◆

1. If you are in the midst of a divorce, make a list of what you want in the divorce settlement based on a thoughtful assessment of the actual conditions and the spirit of generosity.

2. If you are in the aftermath of a divorce, how well did you and your lawyer work together to carry out your wishes? Did it escalate the combat with your ex-spouse, or lead to solutions? Be specific.

3. What choices do you have if you are displeased with the settlement? What are the pitfalls?

4. What are your alternatives if your ex-spouse chooses to return to court?

• 9 •

Friends and Family

◇

And let the best be for your
friend. If he must know the ebb
of your tide,
let him know its flood also.
For it is his to fill your need
but not your emptiness.

—KAHLIL GIBRAN
THE PROPHET

◇

What to Expect

When people talk about their divorces, one of the first things
they bring up is how their friends and family reacted. Friendships are often the real casualties of divorce. After a divorce, it is
not uncommon to miss a friendship more than the ex-husband
or wife.

LOSING FRIENDS HURTS

Losing friends hurts, especially at a time when you may
have had enough of broken relationships and being alone.

"Kate was my best friend," Lidia said. "I couldn't believe it
when she stopped calling me after the divorce and put me off

when I got through to her. Finally we just stopped seeing each other completely. Years later when we talked about it (after *her* divorce), she said her own marriage had been on such shaky ground then that she hadn't wanted to be around anyone who was living out her worst fear—getting divorced. Her husband had also wanted her to break off the contact so that I wouldn't 'draw her into my single lifestyle.' "

DISILLUSIONMENT AS HANGOVER

People often say things like:

- "Where did they all go? I thought they were friends. I guess I can chalk that up to experience!"
- "After all I did for them! Well, I don't need them anyway. They'd better not count on me when the chips are down after how they treated me!"
- "You can't trust anybody. I'll never put that kind of energy into friendship again."

It's easy to feel cynical and disillusioned if friends desert you after the divorce, but like other aspects of the hangover, this is just another way to protect yourself from the pain. In the end, it only keeps you from being open to new friendships and enjoying one of life's greatest pleasures.

WHY FRIENDS FALL AWAY

Divorce disrupts friendship in many ways:

- *The friendships you developed during your marriage were often based on you and your ex-spouse as a couple, not as individuals.* When the marriage breaks up and you become separate people, it is hard for friends to see either of you in this new way. You may have had, or thought you had, individual friendships within your "couple friend-ships," but the relationship they originally chose was one of couples. Now, you are no longer what they chose. They are forced to choose again—this time, with the added baggage of having watched the relationship fall apart, whatever unpleasantness went on during the divorce, and fears about their own relationship.

- *Even single friends will have to make adjustments in how they perceive you.* You are no longer as "safe" and "taken" as you once were. Single friends will have to develop new relationships with both of you, but especially with the partner of the opposite sex.
- *Your friends have experienced a loss, just as you have, and they may have their own hangovers from your divorce.* They have lost you as a couple, and their relationship to you as a couple. They may be angry at you for shattering this part of their lives.

Some people just need a little time to get used to the new picture of you as a single person. Give them the time they need. Don't say, "Well, you didn't support me right from the beginning so I don't want you in my life anymore." Some people come back to only half of the couple; others can remain friends with both of you.

- *Friends may simply not know what to do with you.* Years after my divorce I ran into a woman who had been a close friend before the divorce. She surprised me by saying, "I didn't get in touch with you because every time I saw you, you looked so happy. (Little did she know.) I didn't think you needed me. I figured you were putting together a whole new life."

I had wondered what had happened to her and resisted saying that she could have called me to see if her assumptions were actually true. Some time after that, she went through her own divorce and I made sure to call her.

Think back to times when your friends have gotten divorced. Did you always know what to do? Were you confused about your loyalties, or about how to relate to either party now that both people were single?

THE KINDS OF SUPPORT YOU *DON'T* NEED

You don't need the kind of support that comes from other people's hangovers and feeds yours:

- "I'm so glad you're out of that relationship. How could you have married her in the first place?!"
- "He's the worst. Why do you ever allow him to see the kids? Why don't you get rid of him once and for all?"

These people are fueling the fire, whipping up the old resentments, and providing reasons to keep your hangover alive. They don't usually mean to be unsupportive; they are just caught up in the whirlwind of their own hangovers.

They aren't just going after your ex-spouse; *they are going after you.* Under the guise of supporting you, they are telling you that you're a jerk for ever having been involved with that person. Their criticism may be subtle. They may suggest that your divorce was bad for your children, for instance, with back-handed comments like, "Oh, isn't it too bad you have to take on all that extra work. When do the children get your time? Aren't you tired after a long day at work? How will you have the energy to read them a bedtime story?"

This sounds sympathetic on the surface, but it undermines your ability to do what you have to do, which is to work *and* take care of the children. By allowing people to speak that way in your presence, you are undermining yourself.

Even when their sympathy is heartfelt, it isn't healthy if it casts you in the role of victim or Poor Thing. "You must be exhausted!" "You didn't deserve what she did to you."

Don't buy into this kind of sympathy. It may be a quick fix, but you'll soon discover that you feel tired or depressed whenever you talk to these people. If people can't support you in the way you need to be supported, then they may not get to be around you right now—even if they are close family members.

THE KINDS OF SUPPORT YOU *DO* NEED

Truly supportive people are aware of your needs and feed your energy. They say things like:

- "How are you doing?"
- "Can I take the children for a couple of hours?"
- "Do you need someone to talk to?"
- "You're doing such a great job. Why don't you treat yourself to a sitter and come to see a movie this afternoon?"

They do not take sides, or make anyone right or wrong. They see your strengths and speak to them, rather than heaping on sympathy. You may need a shoulder to cry on from time to time, but then you need someone with whom to brainstorm about what to do next.

The night after my ex-husband and I decided to get divorced, we were to get together with another couple. I called the woman to tell her and, instead of the silence I had feared, she said without hesitation, "If there is anything I can do for you, just let me know. I know this is going to be a hard time. Just remember that I'm here." Her support was immediate, clear, and sincere. I will never be able to repay her for making my initial transition from "couple" to "single" so gentle.

Be around people who love you, think you are terrific, and build your self-esteem. Be selective; sometimes a good book is better company than nonsupportive people.

YOUR EX-IN-LAWS

Your own family members are likely to stick by you—in either productive or unproductive ways—because their first loyalty is to you, but you may lose your relationships with your in-laws. For some people, this is a blessing. For others, it involves real pain.

My ex-mother-in-law and I were very close. She was the only one I talked to when my marriage wasn't working. She said to me, "You are the daughter I never had and I love you to death.

No matter what happens you are still my daughter. He's my son, and you're my daughter." I know she meant that, but after the divorce it must have been too hard for her to keep up the connection and we lost one another.

We often marry the other person's family as much as the person, especially when we marry young. This bond isn't always recognized, but it is very powerful and those people can be a painful loss.

If you want to continue your relationships with your in-laws, give them every opportunity to stay connected with you, but keep in mind that their first loyalty is to your ex-spouse. How they treat you is one of the best indications of where your ex-spouse is with his or her hangover. If the other person has healed, he or she will tell the family to stop ostracizing or criticizing you, *and they will.* If it continues, your ex-spouse is either allowing it or encouraging it.

YOUR OWN FAMILY

When you divorce, your parents lose the security of knowing that their child is safe and being cared for by a mate, surrounded by the tidy package of home, family, hearth, and fire.

Because they love you, this frightens them. They may want to put all the pieces back together again and force the marriage to work. But when they can't do that, they feel helpless and frustrated. Sometimes they even feel responsible. If they had raised you differently, or if they had treated your ex-spouse differently, maybe you wouldn't be getting a divorce.

They may take out their frustration on your ex-spouse, or on you. Their criticism is often indirect, and often it reflects their own hangovers or hangups.

- *What they say:* "She was never any good; you should have gotten rid of her years ago."
- *What they mean:* "I've been so worried. You were always so stupid about women, and now my worst fears have come true. What did I do wrong?"

- *What they say:* "Will you be able to manage with just your salary?"
- *What they mean:* "You? My little Jane (or my little Jack)? Out in the world all alone? You'll be eaten alive! We can't support you for*ever*. Maybe you'd have done better if we'd sent you to a different school!!"

Your family are often the people you turn to first and lean on most. Be aware that they may have their own hangovers, and don't let them fuel yours.

SEPARATING THE WHEAT FROM THE CHAFF

Divorce separates the wheat from the chaff, the true friends of real value from those you might as well let go. The true friends will be there for you once they come to terms with the situation, and you may be surprised at who your true friends are.

The new friends you make will be more valuable because they will teach you about the new person you are becoming. You will learn what qualities you like and value now, and what new things you want from friendship.

7 Strategies for Dealing with Family and Friends

Now that you know what to expect, use these seven strategies to manage your relationships with friends and family during and after the divorce:

1. Let friends and family know as soon as possible that you are getting a divorce.

I called my friends immediately because I didn't want them to hear about it from someone else. Being married is like belonging to a club, and I wanted to tell them that dropping my membership had nothing to do with them, or with the club itself.

I felt better about myself because I handled it that way, and anything you can do to feel better about yourself in this vulnerable time is important.

Telling your friends is also a way to take action, rather than sitting around worrying about what to do. You are moving the process forward. You are making it more real in your own mind by telling others, and that is the first step to healing.

2. Don't write your friends off; take the initiative and reach out to them.

You need their support more now than ever. Even though this is a confusing time and you may be afraid of their reactions, stay in touch with your friends unless they make it clear that they need some distance.

Don't assume they have pulled away just because they don't call you. Give them the benefit of the doubt.

Gene sat back and waited to see who would get in touch with him after the divorce. He waited and waited, and very few people did. They were hearing about it from other people, wondering why he hadn't called, and assuming he was in terrible shape since they hadn't heard from him. They didn't want to intrude on his obviously troubled state of mind.

Meanwhile, Gene was sitting by the phone making wholesale decisions about what rotten friends they had been, how he didn't need them anyway, and how maybe he'd move to another town where people didn't head for the hills at the first sign of trouble.

It may not be fair that you have to make the first move when you're already struggling to stay afloat emotionally and possibly financially, but you are the one with the most to gain or lose. If you want to keep these relationships intact or at least give them the best possible chance of surviving, you have to take charge and direct the action, much as you would with your children.

3. Don't make your friends choose sides.

Soon after his divorce, a man I knew came running up to me at a party shouting, "If you continue to see my wife, you are no longer a friend of mine! Make up your mind right now."

Divorce seems to transform some people into seven-year-olds. They say things like, "If you're friends with *him*, you can't be friends with *me!*" or "What were you doing over at *her* house on Friday?" It seems to them that anyone who remains friends with their ex-spouses is making a statement that the ex-spouses were right about everything and that they were wrong.

Pressuring your friends to choose sides isn't fair to them and may result in their not being friends with either of you. If they are constantly subjected to diatribes against your ex-spouse, if you are always complaining, justifying your actions, or trying to drive a wedge between them and your ex-spouse, they will almost certainly be uncomfortable and may not want to spend time with you.

The divorce is between you and your ex-spouse. When you make your friends a battleground for your struggle, the burden is often too great and they aren't willing to carry it.

4. Let them respond honestly.

As hard as this may be, you have to allow your friends and family their genuine responses to your divorce. These reactions will range from anger, to pity, to fear, to genuine support, to all of the above—both for you and for your ex-spouse.

You don't have to sit and hold their hands as they work through each emotion, but you do have to let them be wherever they are. Some people need to talk to you, ask questions, and vent their feelings. Before you do this, ask yourself whether you feel strong enough, and whether the relationship is worth putting your own internal work aside for the moment. You may want to do this with your mother or closest friends, but not with the dry cleaner or your father's Aunt Louella.

Put yourself first, but keep in mind that other people need to work through their own losses in their own ways.

5. Coach them in how to support you.

Again, remember your own confusion when friends got divorced. Should you call them? What should you say? Should you be sympathetic, or were they trying to keep a stiff upper lip? You probably wanted to help them, but were looking for clues to how to go about it. Everyone handles crises differently, and you didn't want to do the wrong thing.

Your friends will probably appreciate being coached in how

to support you. You may want different things from different people at different times. Be alert to your own needs, and keep your friends informed. Do you want lots of attention, or would you rather be left alone? Hugs? Phone calls? Cards? Invitations to dinner, the movies, walks? Do you want to talk it out or just share silent company?

Don't be afraid of sounding like a tour director or a drill sergeant. Your friends will be relieved to know what you want and glad to be doing something that really helps.

6. Don't tolerate criticism of your ex-spouse.

One thing you should definitely tell people is that you don't want to hear any criticism of your ex-spouse—or yourself, for that matter. You don't need anything around you right now that might instigate, maintain, or prolong your hangover.

I have a friend who was at the end of her rope dealing with all the emotional upheaval and complicated logistics of the divorce. Her mother was by her side night and day, which was helpful up to a point, but the mother's constant criticism of the ex-husband was making my friend crazy. Finally, she had to say, "Mother, I need your support and I love having someone I can tell that I'm hurt, tired, or scared, but I just can't tolerate any more criticism of Lloyd. If you can't stop, I just can't have you around me anymore."

Friends and family are wonderful barometers of your hangover. If the people around you are critical of your ex-spouse, it is an indication that your hangover is still in place. If they knew you wouldn't tolerate it, they wouldn't do it.

7. Take a philosophical attitude toward friends who fall by the wayside.

If people drift away after the divorce, don't waste time or energy on anger or resentment.

When Claire was divorced, her friends, Alison and Bert, no longer called her to play tennis or have brunch. Alison, who had been one of her closest friends, actually had more trouble with the divorce than Bert did. It was hard for Claire to come to terms with losing Alison's friendship, but somewhat easier to understand why Bert didn't pursue their relationship. He was married to a woman who was now a former friend, and she was now a single woman. Alison would disapprove on several fronts, and Claire understood that he wouldn't want to risk his marriage for the sake of their casual friendship.

Claire's challenge was to become as philosophical about Alison's departure as she was about Bert's. She realized eventually that she deserved more loyal friends than Alison had been, was thankful for what the episode had revealed, and moved forward into deeper and more substantial friendships.

These exercises will help you pinpoint the role that friends and family play in your divorce or hangover.

SUMMARY

- Friends and family are often the real casualties of divorce.

- Remember that friends and family may have their own hangovers from your divorce. Don't let their unfinished emotional business fuel yours.

- *Supportive* friends and family will be concerned about both parties' well-being, and genuinely want to help you through this difficult time without casting you in the role of victim or Poor Thing.

- Keep the divorce between you and your ex-spouse.

- Take the initiative with friends; be the one responsible for maintaining the relationship.

◆

WORKBOOK EXERCISES

◆

1. How did your friends, family, you, and your ex-spouse behave at the time of the divorce and afterward?

2. Are you still carrying bad feelings about certain people's behavior? Explain.

3. Write down the seven strategies for dealing with family and friends and check the ones you have used. Set up ways to cover the others in a reasonable period of time.

4. List friends and family who have been supportive and helpful.

5. List people you haven't seen in a long time who share your interests.

6. List the qualities of the people on these lists that appeal to you. Stay in touch with them.

• 10 •

Your Ex-spouse's Hangover

◇

The sky knows the seasons and patterns
behind all clouds,
And you will know too, when you lift
yourself high enough
to see beyond horizons.

—RICHARD BACH
ILLUSIONS

◇

To keep from getting swept up in your ex-spouse's hangover, you
have to step back, understand its components, and see how it's
put together. You can tell how serious you are about healing
your own hangover by how you deal with his or hers.

It Takes Two

Your hangover and your ex-spouse's are deeply connected
and intertwined. It's almost impossible for one to exist without
the other.

By the same token, if one person heals the hangover, it is
much more difficult for the other to keep his or hers going. A
person with a severe hangover usually goes to extremes to get

170

the other's attention—starting vicious rumors in an effort to get a reaction, by physical assault, or other outrageous behavior. The point is to engage the other person and force him or her back into the game.

THE TANGO: ACTION AND REACTION

Someone takes the first step, and the other reacts with just a bit more emotional charge. Then the first person hits back a little harder, and the chain reaction is set in motion.

Sam arrived at 5:00 on Friday to pick up the children. He rang the doorbell, but nobody answered. He rang again, checked the garage to make sure the car was there, and walked around the house trying to get someone's attention. Finally he banged on the door. It flew open and Gwen greeted him saying, "Hi! How are you?"

"Didn't you hear the doorbell?" he screamed.

"No, we were all upstairs getting ready." Their three daughters were lined up behind her with wary smiles.

"You knew I was coming at 5:00. What do you mean, you were getting ready?"

Gwen could never stand his screaming, especially in front of the children, and began to lose it. He had always been like this—critical, self-centered, inconsiderate.

"Well, I don't know what you're so upset about. I was taking the trouble to pack their things. I was doing this for *you!*"

"You never did *anything* for me," he yelled.

"Well, they're not going with you if you're going to behave like this," she shouted. The argument escalated until Gwen slammed the door in his face and locked it. The wide-eyed children, perhaps because they were on her side of the door, thought that she was a heroine and he was a raving maniac.

It doesn't take much to set the dance in motion, and it doesn't matter who makes the first move. Once the argument begins, it lurches forward on its own energy and you often have trouble even remembering what it was about.

STOP THE MUSIC

It's easy to blame everything on the other person. If he or she didn't do those aggravating things, you wouldn't react. Your ex-spouse may be the one who usually takes the first step, but someone has to stop the music and step off the dance floor— and that person has to be you. If you wait for your ex-spouse to do it, you may wait forever and you'll lose all control over the situation.

How do you stop the music and put an end to the action-reaction dynamic? The first step is to recognize where your ex-spouse's hangover is likely to show up, and be on the lookout so that you don't get drawn in.

Hangover "Hot Spots"

These are the tender areas where your ex-spouse's hangover often flares up, and they are probably your "hot spots" as well. They are similar to the list of "power points" you developed earlier. "Power points" are simply areas in which power can be used positively or negatively. "Hot spots" are the specific areas in which power is, or has been, *abused* in your relationship.

Almost anything that you and your ex-spouse shared can be a "hot spot," but the three most vulnerable areas are usually children, finances, and friends.

CHILDREN

When children are a "hot spot," they often get caught in the crossfire between their parents.

A few months after the divorce, Eric noticed that Dawn, 6, and Daniel, 8, acted shy, withdrawn, and frightened when they came to visit him. He asked them if something was wrong, but they just shook their heads, looked at the floor, and wouldn't talk about it. They seemed particularly quiet and uncomfortable when his girlfriend, Cindy, was around. The four of them had enjoyed a Sunday picnic in the woods and a trip to the zoo together, but suddenly the children started acting as if Cindy and, to some extent, Eric were monsters.

Finally, he took Daniel aside for a talk and found out that his ex-wife, Kim, had been telling the children that Eric didn't love them anymore, that he had moved so he could spend more time with Cindy because he loved her much more than he loved any of them—but that they had to keep visiting him or else he wouldn't give them any more money and they wouldn't have enough to eat. They'd have to move out of the house into a shelter, stop going to school, and might even die before they grew up—all because of Cindy.

Eric was livid. He called Kim and threatened to take her back to court to get custody of the children.

"You haven't seen anything yet!" she screamed. "I'll make sure everyone in town knows about Cindy. I'll tell the kids even worse things, like how you hit me last Christmas and how you've been running around with her for years. I'll get you for every cent you make for the rest of your life! No amount of money could repair what you did to us with that little whore."

"You're a rotten mother!" he shouted. "I should have Cindy come over and teach you a few things."

It went on from there until they actually did go to court. Eric tried to get the children and Kim tried to get more money, but they came away with exactly the arrangement they'd had when they went in—except that every lurid detail of the relationship with Cindy was dragged up, the children had to testify, and all of them felt even worse about themselves and one another.

Eric let himself be swept up in Kim's hangover. When the other person comes after you as viciously as Kim did, and seems to be deliberately trying to damage both you and your children, it's hard to keep a level head. The temptation is to strike back and hurt the other person as much as he or she is hurting you. This is an instinctive, knee-jerk reaction to protect yourself and your children, but it is not the best or healthiest response, either for you or for them.

If Eric had tried to understand the roots of his ex-spouse's behavior, he would have realized that the children were a "hot spot" for Kim. Her own mother had never made her feel loved, and Kim had always doubted her own parenting. When Cindy appeared to be stepping into her place, she felt extremely threatened and fought back by poisoning the children against Eric and Cindy.

Kim's response wasn't fair, right, or healthy, but Eric only made it worse by reacting as he did. Instead, he might have told Kim that he was very concerned about some of the children's attitudes and would like to talk with her about them. He could have told her what Daniel had said and then asked if she'd really meant to give the children that impression, and why. What had he done to prompt that? Did she need to express her anger directly to him? What could he do now to make things better between them so that the children didn't become pawns in their battle?

Even though these questions don't directly address her root fear of being a bad parent, they are conciliatory and non-threatening. In her state of mind, it would have been a mistake for him to presume to tell Kim what was going on with her. His questions might have opened up communication and given her a chance to vent her anger at Eric, instead of taking it out on the children. At the very least, it would have stopped the battle from escalating. With some compassion, generosity, and understanding, he might have saved everyone a great deal of hurt and pain, and set a precedent for future interactions with Kim.

Eric also could have talked to the children about what was going on and trusted that his love was so strong they would feel it no matter what Kim said.

MONEY

Laura let Evan draw her into his hangover in much the same way. Their settlement included modest alimony and child support for their three children, who were 8, 10, and 11. Laura had just reentered the work force as a bank teller. She planned to move up, but for the time being relied heavily on Evan's support. When she started seeing someone after the divorce, Evan's previously hidden hangover raged to the surface. He immediately stopped sending the alimony checks. When she called him, he told her, "Get your new boyfriend to support you. Why should he get it for free?" Soon, even the child support money started to dwindle—first to three-quarters, then to half.

Laura couldn't afford a lawyer, but she was so furious that she hired one anyway and went after Evan. The expense of this process was more than the alimony and child support would have been, and even though she won, he found ways to postpone or minimize the payments. Finally, he just disappeared. He quit his job, left town, and they never found him.

Laura was ruined financially. She had to sell the house and struggle for years before she was back on her feet. The battle had not been worthwhile either financially or emotionally.

Instead of letting her hangover run wild along with Evan's, Laura might have sat down with him and found out why her dating someone else upset him so. It is normal to have twinges when the other person starts dating, but his reaction was extreme. If she had asked, she might have discovered that he always suspected she had had an affair the year after they were married . . . or that he wasn't feeling very good about himself when it came to dating again . . . or that even though he no longer wanted to be married, he was still very attracted to her sexually.

He might not have admitted these things to her, but her questions might have brought some realizations and he might have calmed down. Even if he had ended the discussion after thirty seconds, just making that effort to connect in a respectful, compassionate way—and then *not* going after him with the lawyer—may have helped.

Money "hot spots" are likely to show up in taking the other person back to court for a new settlement in which you either give less or get more; being late with checks; and complaining that the children don't have enough money.

FRIENDS

Lynn and Keith had both been back in the dating pool about six months after their divorce when Lynn started getting strange reactions from their former friends. People stopped talking when she walked into the room, looked at her as if they had a secret they didn't want to share with her, and avoided getting together when she called.

She finally asked a close friend what was going on and learned that Keith had been telling a string of increasingly dramatic and damaging lies about her. He hinted that she abused their young children, had had three or four affairs in the last years of their marriage, and salted away money from their joint account to buy these men expensive presents.

Lynn had no way to fight back. She couldn't put an ad in the paper or make a public announcement that these things weren't true. Instead, she called Keith and read him the riot act. When she did that, he knew he'd won. He'd gotten exactly what he wanted: she was isolated, confused, and upset. When she confronted him, he turned the whole situation around by saying, "What do you mean, I'm making them ostracize you? Are you trying to turn our friends against me?"

This upset her even more. She felt battered and exposed, and just couldn't deal with the situation anymore. She turned against both Keith and the friends, and found a whole new group of people.

Lynn's friends had shown her something about themselves by being so eager to believe what Keith had said, but she might have been able to save those relationships if she hadn't gotten drawn into his hangover and overreacted. She might have been able to sit down with at least some of them and talk through the situation. Instead, she let Keith's hangover be the trigger for throwing all of them away.

7 Strategies for Dealing with Your Ex-spouse's Hangover

Why should you bother to manage your own reactions, or to help ease your ex-spouse's hangover whenever possible? There are two good reasons:

- You avoid the action-reaction dynamic.
- In some ways, the two of you have different forms of the same hangover. Anything you can do to heal the other person also heals you.

You can't force your ex-spouse to heal his or her hangover—that is his or her job, not yours—but neither can you simply write it off as the other person's problem.

If your ex-spouse is at all willing to let go, using these strategies will ease the way:

1. Be compassionate; the other person hurts, too.

It may not look as if your ex-spouse is hurting if he has just run off with his twenty-year-old secretary, or she is honeymooning with her wealthy new husband aboard their yacht in the Caribbean. The other person's pain may not look the same way yours does, and his or her losses may not be the same as yours, but your ex-spouse's losses and pain are just as real as yours—*regardless of who "left" the marriage and regardless of how well he or she has disguised or suppressed the hurt.*

Zack seemed to be having the time of his life after the divorce—hoards of girlfriends, expensive vacations, the new Alfa Romeo, out every night. It made Martha and her friends crazy to think that their marriage had meant so little to him and that he was so delighted to be out of it.

The fact was, Zack was in terrible pain. He missed his children so much that he often cried when he was alone. He hated not living in his old home. He was staying in an apartment because the thought of living in another house, not the one they had shared, was too painful even to contemplate. He was so close to the edge that he tried to put it all out of his mind with the women and fast cars. The only thing that could make things worse, in his mind, was for everyone to *know* how awful he felt.

No one comes through a divorce without pain. Once you understand that the other person's hangover is only a cover-up for that pain, just as yours is, you are in a better position to be compassionate.

2. Don't rub salt in the wounds.

You know what your ex-spouse's "hot spots" are and what would drive that person absolutely crazy. Don't do it! There is no point in rubbing salt in the wounds. Hurting your ex-spouse won't help you; it will only make your own hangover worse.

Al had always been very jealous about Linda, and their marriage ended over an affair she'd had. He was quite punishing in the financial settlement and made sure all their friends knew that they'd broken up because she was such a "whore." Linda was very aware of Al's wounds and furious over the settlement, so she never missed an opportunity to parade her latest date or boyfriend around him. It gave her a fleeting, momentary high to get back at him this way, but later she always felt depressed.

The cheap thrill of revenge isn't worth undoing your progress toward healing the hangover.

If you must discuss areas that are "hot spots"—children or finances, for instance—handle them as gently as possible. Instead of welcoming opportunities to hurt the other person, approach the subject with tact. You might say something like, "I know that this is a tender area for you, but it's something we have to talk about. . . ."

The Golden Rule—acting toward your ex-spouse as you would like him or her to treat you—is not only the right approach here, it's the smart one. It gives you peace of mind, keeps you out of trouble, and you may even get some considerate treatment back from your ex-spouse.

3. Learn to detach—and to stay that way even when your detachment makes the other person crazy.

If you have been working on your hangover, you may be able to stay fairly detached when the other person comes around trying to pick a fight. This is a good sign, but be prepared. Your very detachment may upset the other person and trigger a whole new wave of anger.

Bud hadn't wanted the divorce and was furious when May took the kids and left him. She hadn't worked in the eight years they'd been married and he came up with a plan. The first two months, he sent the full alimony and child support; after that, he cut it back severely, thinking she'd had enough time alone and would come running back.

What he didn't know was that May had turned her hobby of weaving rugs into a business. Over the past year, during her marriage, she had secretly sold three rugs to various craft and specialty shops in the nearby metropolitan area. Each had commanded several thousand dollars and earned her more commissions. A few months after the divorce, she had more work than she could handle, and demand for her rugs made prices soar.

She was doing very well financially—actually far better than Bud was doing—and so not only was she very detached when he cut back the payments, she was actually glad. Bud had become a progressively more violent alcoholic and she had been planning to leave him for some time. She had already dealt with a lot of the losses and changes, so she had very little hangover. She wanted to become financially independent as soon as possible to eliminate that tie to him; her success had just happened more quickly than she'd expected.

When Bud didn't hear from May after sending these minimal payments, he stopped the checks entirely. When he still didn't hear, he got drunk, went storming over to May's house, and banged on the door demanding to see her and the kids. She told him calmly through the door to go away, that she no longer needed his money, that she didn't want to talk to him or have the children see him in that condition. She finally called the police and did what she had to do to protect herself and the children, but she never fought back directly or got caught up in his hangover.

There are three reasons that your ex-spouse may become enraged when he or she doesn't get a reaction from you:

1. He or she may think this means you never cared anyway, and certainly don't now.
2. It means that you are healing and letting go of the relationship, when he or she clearly is not.
3. It deprives your ex-spouse of the only way he or she now has to connect with you or get your attention.

When you don't respond, the other person will turn up the volume. His or her behavior will become more extreme and you may even see some new tactics, things he or she is *sure* will draw you in—embarrassing public brawls, flaunting a new relationship, whatever is most likely to get a knee-jerk reaction from you.

Don't fall for it. If you react, the other person will know that this tactic works and try it again and again. If you stay detached, he or she will eventually have to give up. Taking the high road does not mean keeping the peace at any price. You can't back away from every battle. When something is important to you—your children, their education or safety, your business, etc.—you may have to stand your ground. Save those moments for when you really need them.

4. Be alert to new developments in your and your ex-spouse's hangovers.

The most common and dramatic new development is "the new man" or "the new woman." Regardless of how much healing has been done, there is usually a major or minor jolt when you first see your ex-spouse with someone else, or he or she sees you with someone new.

Gary had been involved with his new wife before he and Bette were divorced and Bette still got livid at the mention of Eve's name. They had been divorced for six months when they and their respective partners were invited to the same cocktail party. The hostess had told Gary that Bette and Curt had been invited to the same cocktail party, but he chose to ignore this veiled warning. If Gary had been more sensitive to Bette's probable reaction to his new circumstances—the marriage to Eve two weeks earlier—he could have avoided the explosive scene that occurred that night. He didn't have to spend the rest of his life avoiding Bette, but this particular encounter was almost guaranteed to be negative. In fact, the two ex-spouses actually ended up in a fistfight!

Some changes to which you may want to be particularly alert are:

- New relationships or the birth of children—yours or your ex-spouse's
- Dramatic changes in the financial picture—yours or your ex-spouse's
- Moves to other parts of the country, especially when this means that one parent won't see as much of the children

5. Recognize what you can and cannot do about your ex-spouse's hangover.

Your ex-spouse's hangover may be so severe that there is nothing you can do about it—at least for now. In extreme cases, he or she may make your life so miserable that you have to move to a new location. Even though this may feel like retreat, take the stance that it is an active decision you've made on your own behalf.

You have to step in when you feel that your ex-spouse's hangover is adversely affecting your children, or your relationship with them. The message you want to get across is: "I know you're very angry with me, but let's not put the children in the middle. We both love them and want the best for them. Let's figure out what that is and make sure they get it."

Don't retaliate by saying something even worse to the children about your ex-spouse. Your children will see the difference between how you're handling the situation and how the other parent is handling it.

You can also encourage your children to speak up. Tell them, "If what your father is saying about me really bothers you, speak up and tell him so. Otherwise, just know that he is working through some stuff and that his reactions have more to do with that, and with me, than they do with you."

If you have to interact regularly with your ex-spouse, you can sit down with him or her and say something like: "You know, we seem to be in a strange relationship now. We loved each other once and that felt wonderful. I always remember that day we took a long walk on the beach and then came home and built a fire (or some other good memory you share). Look how far we've come from that. I'd like for us to be able to treat each other with respect, if not with love."

Try to find out what would make it easier for the other person to bury the hatchet. Is there something that you are doing that is driving him or her crazy? If it's something as minor as not having the children ready on time, perhaps you can make the effort to change. If it's something you aren't able or willing to change—dating new people, living in the same town—at least his or her complaint has been heard. You can say, "I wish I could do something about that, but it's just the way things are."

If the other person is upset that you don't feel worse than you do, or that you are healing your hangover, you might say, "I've felt a lot of pain in the past, but I've been working through it. Sometimes I feel guilty for not feeling worse than I do, but the fact is I'm feeling better about things now."

When you talk about the things he or she does that drive *you* crazy, be sure to avoid blame or fault-finding. Treat it as *your* reaction, not something he or she does to you. Use such messages as, "When you say you don't want to see the children if you can't see them all the time, I feel sad that they're missing the experience of knowing you and having a father in their lives."

Point out that *the two of you* are involved in this experience (parenting the children, dealing with the finances, whatever you are working on), and that you want to find a way of working together so that it is positive for everyone.

You may get an enthusiastic response, or you may get total rejection. You will find your place somewhere on the continuum between best-case and worst-case scenarios. Recognize where you are now and operate from that point of view, even though you hold open the possibility that things will get better in the future.

Mend as many bridges as you can, but remember that all you can do is your best.

6. Work on your own hangover.

This is one place where you have control and can make positive changes unilaterally. Every step you take toward healing your own hangover has the chance of affecting your ex-spouse positively.

7. Let go of expectations about your ex-spouse.

This is the clearest sign that you are healing. When you no longer expect from that person the things you expected during the marriage—having the laundry done, fixing the car, helping yourself to his or her time, bending his or her ear, a shoulder to cry on, financial security, a wonderful home, social status, perfect children—then you know you are coming to the end of the hangover.

These expectations are the material of which hangovers are made, the issues that have controlled your life and dictated your feelings. If the other person met these expectations, you were happy. If he or she didn't, you were upset. You know you've let go when you begin to see your ex-spouse in a neutral, unemotional way.

When you finally let go of those expectations and understand that you—not your spouse, ex-spouse, friends, or family—are responsible for having what you want in your life, you start to become whole again.

SUMMARY

- As long as you and your ex-spouse have contact, you will be part of the dynamic of his or her hangover.

- Only you can choose whether you will be hooked in by your ex-spouse's hangover.

- As long as you and your ex-spouse make judgments about or have expectations of one another, you are still bound together.

◆

WORKBOOK EXERCISES

◆

1. List the issues that touch off your ex-spouse's hangover.

2. How do you respond?

3. Which issues are avoidable between you and your ex-spouse? Which are not?

4. What can you reasonably do about your ex-spouse's hangover? What areas are out of your control?

5. What ways can you work on your own hangover that would positively affect his or hers?

6. Do you judge or have expectations of your ex-spouse? Be specific. Does he or she judge or have expectations of you? Be specific.

• 11 •

Your Next Relationship

◇

"I daresay you haven't had much practice,"
said the Queen "When I was your age, I
always did it for half an hour a day. Why
sometimes I've believed as many as six
impossible things before breakfast."
—LEWIS CARROLL
THROUGH THE LOOKING-GLASS

◇

Someone New

Before you can experience the joys and challenges of having a
new person in your life, you have to clear away any negative
attitudes that may be blocking that next relationship.

TRAPPED IN THE PAST

At a dinner a couple of years ago, I was seated next to a
British actor who suffered from a massive divorce hangover.
When I told him about my work on "divorce hangovers," he
launched into the story of his "perfectly dreadful" divorce and
how his children "had never gotten over it." After five years, they
were still depressed, miserable, and using the divorce as an

excuse for everything from missing school, to drugs, to having abusive relationships of their own.

This man was involved with a lovely woman, but when I asked if they planned to marry, he answered, "I will *never* marry again. It was the worst thing that ever happened to me and I doubt that either I or my children will ever recover. I want nothing to do with the institution of marriage. My children wouldn't hear of it."

He and his children had gone into collusion, adopting an attitude that guaranteed three things:

1. He would never have to risk being hurt again.
2. His children would never have to share his attention with anyone.
3. All of them would have an excuse for any failure or trouble they experienced for the rest of their lives.

It was a perfect example of how a hangover can not only prevent you from committing to a new relationship, but keep you stuck in all areas of life.

WHAT KEEPS YOU STUCK

When people do not draw new relationships into their lives, it is often because they have succumbed to feelings of failure or guilt about the old relationship. These feelings are actually cover-ups for fear and pain. People think they have failed at the marriage, and start to believe either that they are "incapable of having good relationships," or that relationships themselves are no good. In either case, why would they get involved in another one?

The guilt comes from letting everyone down and destroying people's lives—the ex-spouse's, the family and friends, their own, but especially the children's.

Even if they do manage to draw in new people, these feelings of failure or guilt keep the new relationships from working. Then they have further proof of failure.

REMEMBER THE GOOD PARTS

One way to let go of failure and guilt is to remember the good parts of your old relationship. It probably wasn't all bad. It may have been a special time for both of you, even if it didn't last forever. It may have been an opportunity for love, children, companionship, or growth—however uncomfortable—that you could experience with only that person.

ANGER PINBALL

Another obstacle to getting involved in a new relationship—and making it work—is leftover anger from your marriage or divorce. This anger can be triggered when you start seeing someone new and often seems to come from six directions at once, as if you were trapped inside a pinball machine. Some ways it shows up are:

1. Choosing someone just the opposite of your ex-spouse.

If you are still harboring anger toward your ex-spouse, you may believe that all your problems will be solved by having someone completely different. You'll find yourself saying things like:

- "You're so wonderful with the children, and my ex-husband never really had time for them."
- "You love music and dancing, my favorite things; my ex-wife couldn't stand them."
- "You really understand me; my ex thought I was the same person I was fifteen years ago."

You have grown and expanded since you chose your ex-spouse, *but you are still essentially the same person, with many of the same needs and desires.* Your ex-spouse may be out of your life forever, but that doesn't mean the parts of you that were initially drawn to him or her are gone. If the new person has none of those qualities, you may be making a choice *against your ex-spouse* rather than *for yourself.*

By the time of the divorce, Nan was fed up with Monty's aggressive, outgoing, effusive nature. She hated it when he seemed to leap over chairs at a party to pump yet another hand and acted as if he hadn't seen the person in thirty years. Six months later when she met Gordon, she thought that her prayers had been answered in this quiet, reserved, rather shy man. At first, it was great to be able to stick him in a corner at parties and not have to worry about him embarrassing her, but soon his reticence about getting involved and relating to people began to grate on her nerves. She realized that, while she might not want a lampshade-adorned "life of the party," it was important to her to be with someone who could hold his own socially.

Nan realized that choosing someone whose most striking feature was that he was *not Monty* was a denial of parts of herself. Seeing this dynamic brought home the importance of forgiving Monty and acknowledging the positive things he had brought into her life.

2. Reacting to the new person as if he or she were your ex-spouse.

Unresolved anger always finds a way to explode, and your new love may take the heat for years of your ex-spouse's aggravating behavior.

Steven always hovered over Dinah while she was cooking dinner, "trying to help," but in fact mentally tapping his foot because he wanted the meal to be ready fifteen minutes ago. "Are the peas done yet? Did you put the bread in the oven? Are you going to make a dressing for the salad?" One of the greatest joys of her divorce was being able to move around the kitchen without bumping into him.

The first time she cooked dinner for her new love, Gil, he casually wandered into the kitchen to give her a hug. Not realizing that he was right behind her, she turned and nearly spilled gallons of boiling water and pasta over both of them. She lost it, started screaming, and poor Gil got bombarded with years of hoarded anger over Steven's impatience.

If the repeated behavior is something that you absolutely cannot tolerate—alcoholism, theft, abuse, etc.—then this is definitely a red flag. If it is something relatively minor, just recognize it as a trigger and work on releasing the anger.

Hilary's ex-husband used to throw the Sunday paper all over the living room floor as he read. He would lie on the sofa and, as he finished each section, toss it back over his head onto the rug in an untidy pile of wrinkled newsprint. What Hilary inferred from this, based on the whole history of their relationship and also on her mother's history with her father, was: "I'm the man of the house, smarter and more important than you are, and have the right to do anything I want, even if it makes more work for you. I expect you to keep this house immaculate, and I'm going to sit here and deliberately make life more difficult for you."

The first time she spent Sunday morning with her new love, Miles, and he let a few sections of the paper slide to the floor, Hilary saw red. She let him have it for everything her ex-husband had done to her and everything her father had done to her mother. Fortunately, Miles understood what was happening and invited her to talk about it.

She sat down and told him what she was feeling, and what the real source of her anger was. He reassured her that he did not share those condescending and demeaning viewpoints. She was willing to work through her anger, and he volunteered to be more careful with the paper so that he wouldn't trigger her unnecessarily.

Anger pinball works in reverse, too. Your new love may sometimes relate to you on the basis of what happened with his or her ex-spouse. Often these reactions are completely unconscious, but you might ask the other person if his or her violent reaction to a neutral situation has anything to do with the ex-spouse.

If you both can stay alert to these dynamics, not take them personally, and support one another in working through them, you can put your new relationship on firm ground and build a solid basis for handling future difficulties. If you can't do that, then you will both continue to bump up against these triggers and abandon relationships, bump up against them again and leave again.

The more aware you become of where your triggers are, the better you can manage them and release them, and the better your chances of making a new relationship work.

ESCAPE, OR THE REAL THING?

Be careful not to slip back into the Cinderella or Prince Charming myths. Don't expect your new relationship to guarantee your future or make life perfect. The new person comes to you with all that is wonderful and infuriating about being a human being—just as you come to him or her.

Is the new relationship too much, too fast? Escape from loneliness, or the real thing? There is no rush. If either of you wants to see who else is out there, take some time to date around. If the relationship is right for you, it will still work out. You have come too far to jump into a relationship just to have someone at your side or to keep you from feeling lonely.

Creating Your New Relationship

Your list of personal "power points" from Chapter 5 can be your best tool for creating a healthy, equal partnership. If your new relationship looks promising, I strongly suggest sitting down with the new person in your life and creating a power contract. This contract is nothing like the traditional prenuptial agreement, which anticipates failure. The prenuptial agreement is based on mistrust and fear that the other person will take the money and run; this contract is based on goodwill and mutual respect, so it is much less likely to be broken. With a power contract, you say, "I expect this relationship to succeed, and I am willing to talk about some uncomfortable areas *before the fact* in order to make sure that it *does* succeed. I am in this relationship for the long term, and I want to be sure we both know what we're getting into."

Countless people have said to me during a divorce, "I wish it were harder to get *into* marriage, and easier to get *out!*" The purpose of this contract is to bring up issues *before* you get married, so that you go into it with your eyes open.

In the first rush of love, it may feel awkward or silly to sit down together and talk about these issues—let alone actually write down your responses and expectations. You may be tempted to assume that things will always be as wonderful as they are today, but we have all learned that even the best relationships need attention and nurturing.

When people scoff at actually drawing up a written contract, I ask them: *Why would you expect this relationship to be any better than the last one if you don't make changes?* Often their reluctance to be specific about these points reflects an unhealed hangover.

Use that first blush of love to your advantage. You may never be more eager to listen to one another, or to see things from the other person's point of view.

THE POWER CONTRACT

Using the "power points" list from Chapter 5, talk about each item on your list—finances, children, time, sex, home, social life, religion, privacy, personal habits, and whatever special items appeared on your personal list—and write down:

- How each of you feels about that item
- How important it is to you
- What you expect from the other person in this area
- What he or she expects from you

Then write down:

- What your expectations of the marriage are
- What your expectations of your mate are
- What your mate's expectations of the marriage are
- What your mate's expectations of you are

DON'T GUESS; ASK!

You may think you know what the other person's answers will be, or what *your* responses will be. You may assume *they* know *your* answers. *Don't assume anything; ask, and write down the answers*. Your answers may be different in this relationship from what they were in another.

You may think, "But we'll never get married! We'll never come to terms!" Good! Better to find out now and start working on solutions.

- Stuart learned that Grace did not expect to cook dinner for him every night, as he had assumed she would.
- Angela discovered that Warren expected to spend every holiday with his large family in Georgia.
- Tony had wrongly assumed that Fay would convert to Catholicism when they married because she had been going to church with him and seemed to like it.
- Maggie found that the men in Daryl's family had always visited prostitutes on a regular basis and that he expected to do the same. She decided she couldn't live with that and they chose not to get married.

Stay flexible. Items that were very important a year ago may not be at all important now, and items that weren't even on the list then may have become top priorities.

The smell of garlic made me sick for much of my life, but something must have happened to my olfactory nerves when I was divorced because I started eating a little garlic and liked it. Then I started eating more garlic and loved it. I married a man who is half-Italian and now I eat a *lot* of garlic. If I had put *"no garlic"* on my list and stuck to it rigidly, I couldn't have married this man.

Rework your contract regularly, and always when new circumstances or conditions arise. If you are a two-income couple and one of you decides he or she needs a sabbatical, what do you do? How will children affect the picture? What if one of you becomes chronically ill, or wins the lottery?

Use this contract to support your relationship, to make sure that both of you are communicating and getting your needs met, and that the balance of power stays on an even keel.

YOUR EX-SPOUSE'S GHOST

What role should your ex-spouse play in your new relationship? *None.* The only business your ex-spouse has in your life now is in connection with parenting your children when the children are not with you, or managing whatever other unavoidable responsibilities you still share. Any power or participation in your life beyond that point is not healthy, and will not occur unless you encourage or allow it.

It's not the job of the new person in your life to beat your ex-spouse off with a stick; it is your responsibility to see that he or she stays away and does not interfere in the new relationship.

Two unhealthy ways your ex-spouses can be brought into the new relationship are:

1. *The ex-spouse is played off against the new partner.* In this dynamic, a man plays his ex-wife off against his new wife or partner, or a woman plays the two men off against one another. The person in the middle gets a real ego boost with two people fighting over him or her, but it is destructive to everyone involved, and to all the relationships.
2. *The ex-spouse is invited or allowed to act as commentator on the new relationship.* Either as a "friend of the couple" or as an "outside consultant" to one partner, the ex-spouse is encouraged to get involved in the new relationship, asked his or her opinion about how it's going, and given the right to criticize you, your new partner, or the relationship itself. Now your new relationship has a judge and jury—one who is hardly impartial, and may not have much interest in seeing it succeed.

You can't allow these behaviors to start or to continue. Your new partner would have to be a saint not to feel jealous and threatened. You shared a sexual relationship, a history, and perhaps children with your ex-spouse. Your new partner needs to feel secure and to believe that your allegiance, sympathy, and support are with *him or her* now, and not with your ex-spouse.

IF YOU ARE THE EX-SPOUSE

The same rule applies: *There is no room for triangles in any of these relationships.* New relationships need room to grow. Don't get swept up in the dynamic between your former partner and his or her new spouse.

They may try to put you in the middle and have you resolve their fights, or make you the whipping boy for their problems. It's up to you to say, "Hey, I'm not responsible for your marriage working or failing. I have nothing to do with your relationship. You have to work this out between the two of you."

That doesn't mean that, once everyone's hangover is well under control and you all start acting like grownups, you have to pretend that your ex-spouse dropped off the face of the earth. You can talk with him or her about the children if you need to do so, write a note if his or her parent dies or some other milestone event occurs, and generally behave with kindness and consideration.

◆

SUMMARY

- Leftover guilt and anger can be obstacles in forming new, healthy relationships.

- Discussing expectations about one another and about marriage is your best guarantee of future compatibility and fulfillment.

- A new relationship has no room for former mates.

◆

◆

WORKBOOK EXERCISES

◆

1. Make a "wish list" describing your ideal mate.

2. What qualities, interests, or behaviors of your ex-spouse were incompatible with yours?

3. What qualities, interests, or behaviors of yours were hard to live with?

4. How have you changed since your former relationship?

5. What pluses do you bring to a relationship?

6. Sit down with your new partner and list, independently of one another: your expectations of the new relationship, your "power points," and how both of you will approach each issue. Discuss any behaviors that echo a former spouse's. Discuss these and any other incompatibilities and see if they can be worked out in ways that are satisfactory to both of you.

· 12 ·

Your New Relationship
and Your Children

◇

Let me not pray to be sheltered from dangers
but to be fearless in facing them.
Let me not look for allies in life's battle field
but to my own strength.

—TAGORE
"FRUIT-GATHERING"

◇

A New Family

Each time you introduce a new person into your circle, the family dynamic becomes more complex. The opportunities for hangover flare-ups increase, but you also get even greater rewards in terms of love and growth.

Let's look first at the situation in which you have children but your new partner does not.

WHERE IS THE CENTER OF YOUR UNIVERSE?

Now you have on the table not only your own and your children's hangovers, but also whatever hangover your new partner may have from a previous marriage or even from his or her family of origin. The ball of wax is getting bigger.

You and your new partner are the adults in the new family, regardless of blood ties, traditional roles, or underlying family structure; and no matter how complicated things get, the two of you must present a united front and create the center of your new universe. You have to keep your feet beneath you and stay balanced, because it's your responsibility together to make sure that everyone *else* stays balanced. Without the solid center, everyone (including the two of you) will be confused about where they fit and the new family will begin to splinter.

But as a parent and a lover you alone have the deepest connection to everyone concerned. For that reason, you have the added responsibility to reach out and smooth the way, find out what people's needs and feelings are and make sure they get expressed.

You are extraordinarily lucky if your new partner is as alert to these needs and responsibilities as you are, but don't count on this being the case. The other person may be a quick learner if you get him or her started diplomatically, but again, don't count on it.

You also have to take care of yourself. The more you do for all of them, the more you must do for yourself. At some point, you may have to step back and say, "Listen, *I* need some understanding here. I'm struggling, too. I know it's hard right now but we all have to help each other until we get used to the new situation. We have to be grown-up and make this thing a healthy, positive experience."

You may not always be a perfect tower of strength for either your new partner or your children, and you don't have to hide this from them. Let them know that you need hugs as much as they do, and that you are counting on them to be patient and understanding as much as they are counting on you.

Pamela had some difficulty building bridges between her children and her new husband, Scott. He had not been married before and was not entirely comfortable with young people. The children were very close to their father, who had not remarried. Pamela organized all sorts of family picnics and outings, coached Scott in how to get close to the children, and spent a lot of extra time talking about him to them and laying the groundwork for their new connections. But she also needed time for herself. If she had an hour a day to read, meditate, or just lie down quietly and close her eyes, she felt recharged. She set this time from 4:30 to 5:30 each day, and no one could disturb her during that hour. It was the way Scott and the children supported her in supporting them.

Remember, you are the main beneficiary of investing this time and energy. You get to have your new relationship and feel good about how your children are doing with the new situation.

WHO'S ON FIRST?

Your children have already been through one major change. Now they are being asked to accept another major change, a new person in the family that has included only you and them since the divorce.

Instead of having you at home every night, or always spending weekends only with you, they now have to share you with someone else. Sometimes this new person is also included in picnics, holidays, and other activities that used to be "just family."

You need to address these issues directly and acknowledge that you are asking them to do something big. Don't just hope that they understand what is happening or expect that they will hand you over gladly to the new person.

Tell them that you are getting to know someone new and that they will be getting to know him or her, too. The new person will be spending more time with all of you and be involved in some of their activities. Explain that you may not be around every night, that there will be times when you and the new person may go out of town together, or want to be alone, but that you don't love them any less.

Present the situation as a positive experience, rather than a negative one. It is a chance for them to have a new adult friend who loves them. Make them feel *included* in the relationship, rather than *excluded*.

You might say, "Yes, we'll lose some of our time together, but this person is going to be a new friend. Our family got smaller after the divorce, and now it's going to get bigger again. Just as you make new friends in school, now I'm making some new friends. And just as you like me to meet your new friends, I want you to get to know my new friend."

Ask them how they feel about all of this, but be clear that they are not the ones who call the shots; you are.

Don't leave anything to their imaginations, or allow them to remain confused or ambiguous about what is happening. Give them all the information you can, answer their questions fully, and keep the lines of communication open.

THE INTRUDER

Remember, one of children's greatest fears at the time of the divorce is that you are going to leave them, just as the other parent did. Now someone has come on the scene who threatens to take you away. Consciously or unconsciously, the new partner is often seen as an intruder who is going to destroy what little remains of their family.

This fear can manifest in a variety of ways, depending on the children's ages. At any age, they can be rude. "You have a funny face." "Why do you dress like that? My daddy never dresses like that."

Or they can be coldly polite, refusing to open up at all, or so sullen and furious that they can barely contain themselves. "Hello, Mrs. Smith," they say, and then speak in monosyllables or refuse to say another word for the next three hours. New partner: "Do you like school this year?" Child: "No." New partner: "How's your soccer team doing?" Child: "Okay."

They may also make pointed remarks about how wonderful their other parent is, especially in comparison to the new partner. To the new man, who drives a Toyota, they say, "My father has a Mercedes." To the new woman, "My mother doesn't have any gray hair."

All of these behaviors are reactions to feeling threatened. Their lives are out of control again. They are sick and tired of this, and ready to fight back. Both you and your new partner have to reinforce their feelings of security and make sure they know that the new partner has no intention of taking you away from them.

Children aren't particularly interested in the fact that this person makes you feel good. They don't care if you're having the time of your life; they want to know how this person affects *them*. Reassure them that nothing is being taken away from their lives; something is being added.

In rare cases, children will stonewall and absolutely refuse to accept your new partner. If you have tried your best to make them feel secure and loved, and to present the new person in a positive way, then that's all you can do. Stonewalling suggests a severe hangover, and you may want to consider getting that child professional help.

DOES HE OR SHE LIKE YOUR CHILDREN?

What about your new partner's feelings? Some people love children across the board, others are put off by them, and still others like only their own children.

In the beginning, your new partner may be quite warm and friendly, but after a while the children may start to get on his or her nerves and you'll begin to hear, "Do we really have to take the kids again?"

The new person is just getting to know you and wants to enjoy the intensity of any new relationship. It's natural for him or her to want more time alone with you and, again, it's important to address the issue. When you start getting questions or veiled complaints about including the children again, don't fly off the handle and scream, "Love me, love my children!" Be sensitive to your new partner's needs. You might say something like, "I have the same feeling. I wish we could disappear for six months and be alone, but I just can't do that. I love these children and I'm responsible for them. How can we work things out so that you and I have enough time, but so that the children won't feel left out?"

If the new person can't deal with this, you have some important information about him or her.

YOUR NEW PARTNER'S PARENTING

This is another opportunity for fireworks. Your new partner may not like the way you parent. You may not like the way he or she parents. The new person may think the children should eat at 5:00, so you can get them to bed and have your own time together, that you are overindulgent, or too strict, or should make the children do more around the house, or encourage them to get involved in sports more, or any number of things that make you want to scream, "Back off! These are *my* children!"

They are your children, but if your new partner is living in the same house, some accommodations need to be reached. You have to agree where the balance lies, and both of you have to be consistent with the children.

Some people move more naturally into the role of parent than others. A man may say, "Listen, Johnny, stop giving your mother a hard time," or a woman may rush to the child who has fallen and hurt himself. Others hold back. They may even appear to be stiff and uncaring, but they may just be uncertain about how much involvement you want from them in your children's lives. They may not run to the child who trips because they don't want to invade or interfere.

You have to determine what level of involvement is comfortable for you—and make sure both your new partner and the children know the new ground rules. But you can't assume all the responsibility of parenting like a lion wrapping its paws around its young; if you are serious about creating a new family, then the new partner must play some role.

CHILDREN'S POWER PLAYS

It's important for you and your new partner to be clear about where the responsibility and authority are in the family, because children often swoop in to grab power wherever there is a void. With someone new in the household, the power structure is once again in transition. Since the children are feeling especially vulnerable, they will be on the lookout for ways to leverage power with you and your new partner. These are a few tricks they may try:

- *The Wicked Stepmother or Stepfather.* They visit the other parent and complain about you and your new partner, wailing about how terrible you are together, how miserable their lives have become, how unmercifully they are treated, and how they just want to run away.

  Your ex-spouse questions you about what is going on in the new household and, consciously or unconsciously, you may back off and give the kids more leeway. Now they have concern and sympathy from your ex-spouse, and more power over you.

- *"You ruined my life, so you owe me."* Because you ruined their lives by getting divorced, you now have to give them anything they want.

  Madeline and Kent were married a year after his divorce. His son, Ethan, and her daughter lived with them in the co-op that he had shared with his ex-wife, Elise. Elise, who had severe problems that went beyond the divorce, had never accepted the new marriage and had poisoned Ethan against Madeline.

  One Christmas Madeline and her daughter were going out to take a walk after dinner. Elise was waiting outside their building. She attacked Madeline with an umbrella and pulled out some of her hair, screaming, "Whore! What are you doing, living in my house? It's *mine!*"

  The doormen finally pulled Elise off Madeline, who walked back into the lobby, only to find Kent and Ethan walking toward them. Ethan said, as if his mother had told him what would happen, "This is my house. You don't belong here."

  Later, Kent told Madeline that he thought it best if she started making some other living arrangements.

Kent obviously had many issues, but one was that he felt so guilty about the divorce that he let his son have his way, at the expense of his new relationship.

NEW BOUNDARIES

In healthy families, the adults make the rules and the decisions. The children are satellites; they revolve around the two parents, but *do not come between them*. When alliances evolve so that children are playing the parents off against one another, something is not right.

If children have been used to having this kind of leverage in your former marriage, they will try it again with you and your new partner. Now is the time to stop it. You are already involved in forming new boundaries, guidelines, and relationships. Let them know, without making them feel rejected, that their place is not *between* you and your new partner, but *around* you.

This is also a good chance to work with them on their hangovers, which is what prompts them to try leveraging power. They feel out of control, and so they are grasping at straws, straining for what shreds of power they think they can gather to them. The keys are to recognize this behavior when it occurs, sit down with your children, and talk about what is going on.

You may also want to talk to your new partner and let him or her know that you don't find your children's behavior acceptable, that you are working on it with them, and that you appreciate his or her support. You might say, "I really appreciate the fact that you are being so understanding and sympathetic about this. Maybe you can be more objective and give me some suggestions about how I could work with them."

Be prepared for your new partner to feel left out, hurt, or unsupported because you have not yet built a history together. At times, you or your new partner—whoever is the new person in the family—may need to lean over backward to feel part of the new situation.

THE NEW BALANCE

Everyone has to find his or her place in the new family balance that includes your new partner. You can help the children express their fears and make sure they feel secure, you can help your new partner ease into the family dynamic, but you can't always be the go-between. At some point, the new person and your children have to find their own ways of relating to each other.

Your new partner will bring his or her own emotional baggage to the household, and both you and your children will have to deal with that. You can't always make excuses for the new person ("He was just cross because he was feeling tired.") or for the children ("Give them time; it's only been a year.").

If you always set yourself up as the mediator, you'll be stuck with that role forever. You'll exhaust yourself and start to resent all of them. Worse, they will never learn to work things out for themselves.

You have to trust both your new partner and your children to be the people you love, wonderful people who are facing a lot of changes and challenges right now, but who are strong and open enough to find their own balance and build their own relationship. They may surprise you; what they find together may be more wonderful than anything you could have imagined.

Blended Families

When your new partner also has children and you blend the two families, the hangover possibilities increase exponentially. Now the ball of wax is huge. You can't just put one roof over two families and expect it to work; you have to create a whole new entity.

THE FAMILY TREE

You may now be dealing not only with yourself and your children, your new partner and his or her children, but also with your ex-spouse, that person's new partner and whatever children he or she may have, your new partner's ex-spouse, his or her new partner and whatever children he or she may have, and to some extent with all the grandparents, sisters, brothers, cousins, uncles, aunts, nieces, nephews, and cocker spaniels.

Some of these elements are fairly distant from you, but they all have a way of rippling through and affecting your life. The old saying, "You're not marrying the person; you're marrying the family," was never more true. The potential for chaos and confusion is now enormous.

Fortunately, there is nothing new here; it is just more of the same—lots more. One thing is guaranteed: *If there is anything that hasn't come up before, it will come up now.*

As long as you know from the start that it's not going to be easy, and remember everything you have learned about dealing with the hangover, you will be fine. This is just the next level of challenge.

ROMAN CANDLES

Blending families can be as beautiful, and feel as out of control, as the roman candles at a fireworks show. First there are only the two of you—you and your new partner—working out all the emotional pyrotechnics. Then you add one set of children, then the other, then the ex-spouses and whatever new involvements and children they have. Each person in this brilliant display can set off flares in every other person's hangover until you have a show that eclipses the Fourth of July.

You have some measure of control over your own children, but that is about as predictable as it gets. You don't have a track record with most of these people; you are starting from scratch with a whole new family. You will have to be more aware, more generous, and more responsible than ever before.

TWO STYLES OF PARENTING

Two equally loving, intelligent people can have radically different styles of parenting. You may have different ideas about discipline, how much time adults and children should spend together, and how involved parents should be in their children's lives.

You have no idea how rigid your system is until you try to blend it with someone else's.

What if you've always kept the bedroom door open at night so that you could hear the children cry, and your new partner won't hear of such a thing? Little quirks like this can send thundering messages to children. If they're used to the door being open and suddenly it's closed, they will not see this as a conflict between two styles of parenting. They will think: *My parent never shut the door before; now he or she is closing me out.*

What makes it even harder is that, whatever style of parenting you've used, it has kept you going since the divorce. It has worked for you; why should you change?

These are things that you and your new partner have to work out between you. Again, it's important that you agree on whatever compromises you make, and that you present a united front to the children.

BLENDING CHILDREN

It can be challenging for your children to join with their stepsiblings in a new and larger family. Everyone has to give up his or her old status, routines, and patterns of relating, and find a new place in the group. The "oldest child" may not be the oldest child anymore. The "baby" may not be the baby. The only boy may no longer be the only boy.

Competitions may develop between some children as everybody struggles to find a new place in what appears to be a game of musical chairs. Other children may withdraw from the battle rather than engage in this kind of rivalry. Everyone will be very aware of what privileges are allowed to whom, what restrictions are placed on whom, and how blending the families has changed his or her place in the pecking order.

You have to ride herd on the situation, be alert to trouble spots, provide an opportunity to talk things out, start building connections between the two families, and do whatever you can to ease the transition. Present it as a positive opportunity to enjoy more brothers and sisters, but also acknowledge that it is a challenge and that your children will be bigger people for taking it on.

In our situation, my new husband's children, Wendy, Christy, and Ted, were all older than my two, Jad and Beau, with a nine-year difference between the oldest and the youngest. When the age spread is this wide, there can be differences in the children's interests and capabilities. I made extra sure Beau could keep up when we went skiing or out to dinner, or played a game as a family.

In our case, Wendy remained the oldest, Beau remained the youngest, and Christy remained in the middle. The two who had to change birth order were the two boys. Jad went from being the oldest and the only boy to being the second youngest with an older brother. Ted went from being the baby to being a middle child.

The logical place to look for competition was between the two boys, Ted and Jad, but it never developed. They were very different personalities and had different interests, but they shared a sense of humor and were both excited about having a brother for the first time. They have been closer at some times than others, but the lesson we learned was: Don't go looking for trouble where it may not exist.

One relationship that became challenging was between Wendy, the oldest, and Jad, who had been the oldest. She instinctively knew that she had to hold her territory as "first child" in the new, blended family. Jad had to learn to back off.

The other challenge was between Ted, who had been very secure in his role as the youngest, and the "new youngest," Beau. Ted had liked being the baby very much and resented losing that position to Beau. This led to an incident when he split her lip. This could have established a dangerous precedent if I hadn't immediately taken him aside and made it clear that this behavior was not going to be tolerated.

I was able to do that because I had invested some time and energy in my relationship with Ted prior to the incident. We had gone out to lunch, just the two of us, and had a wonderfully honest conversation. I'd told him, "You know, it's not going to be easy. I'm this new person and you have a sense that you like me, but you don't really know me that well. There will be times when I do things you won't like. We need to know that we can be honest with each other. I care for you but that doesn't mean I won't do things that make you angry. If I do, we should talk about it. Please don't hold on to it. Let me know if you're upset with me."

He knew from that point forward that I was not a threat to him, that I was on his side and honestly wanted to know what he was feeling. Because we had made that connection, I could step right into the situation. I didn't have to go to Roger and say, "Go talk to your son."

Gender and birth order are potential problem areas, but you can never completely predict where the clashes will occur. You just have to stay on top of the situation day to day, and encourage people to talk—to you and to one another.

BUILDING BRIDGES

Building bridges between the two families may mean:

- Finding activities like skiing, tennis, movies, or camping that you all enjoy and can do together.
- Encouraging two of the children who are both interested in a subject like art to take a drawing class together.
- Mediating arguments occasionally, or suggesting that two people who are not talking about their conflicts and resentments do so.
- Making time for your new partner and your children to do things together, perhaps without you, so that they can get to know one another.
- Talking to your own children about the fact that you need to spend some special time with your new partner's children so that you can develop your own relationships with them.

My children were wonderful in this area. I told them very directly, "Listen, I'm working on reaching out and building bridges among all of us. Wendy, Chris, and Ted don't know me, so I want to spend some time with them and develop a trust between us. You know me and you know that I will love you all your life and that I'll always be there. But right now I have to give them a little more attention. I know you'd rather have all my attention, and often I'd prefer to give all my attention to you, but that's not what we're putting together here and I count on you to understand that and support the new family."

They did just that, and made my job of building bridges much easier.

THE FAMILY FORUM

Getting together as a group to talk about how things are going, to discuss any problems that have arisen, and to find solutions can be invaluable for blended families. These meetings are not bitch sessions or casual dinners at which you talk about what happened that day (as important as those dinners may be); they are a forum for the blended family members to get to know one another and work things out.

For family meetings to work, both parents have to be behind the idea and support everyone in participating. Ideally, everyone would be enthusiastic about contributing, but often even members who aren't excited about sitting down with the new family come around when both parents set the tone.

There are too many people involved in a blended family, too many hangovers, and too many individual quirks and problems, to make any assumptions. Just because you don't hear frying pans crashing over heads or fists being put through walls, you can't assume that everything is okay with everyone. Family meetings are a chance to air concerns before they develop into enormous problems, and to talk about ways the family has grown together.

Amanda, 13, asked at a meeting why Cass, 15, got to stay out until midnight on weekend nights when she had to be home by 10:00. She didn't think that two years should make all that much difference. This was actually a bit of a power play, since Amanda's father was a much stricter parent than Cass's mother, who was more relaxed about curfews, room cleaning, etc.

The two parents promised to discuss this discrepancy that night and to get back to Amanda and Cass the next day with their answer. Amanda was delighted, not just at the prospect of having a later curfew, but that she'd had a chance to be heard and get some official consideration for her request.

The older, wiser Cass brought up the fact that the garden of the house to which they had all moved had grown over. She wondered if it would be okay if she replanted it and asked if anyone wanted to help. Amanda, flushed from her curfew triumph, volunteered and this became a bond between the two girls. (Amanda kept her 10:00 curfew, but wasn't too upset because she felt her place in the family was more secure and she was beginning to enjoy her new older sister more.)

5 GUIDELINES FOR FAMILY MEETINGS

Your family meetings shouldn't be overly rigid, but these guidelines will keep them moving in productive directions:

1. Have the first meeting a few months after the two families came together.

The purpose of this meeting is to set the tone of future meetings, establish family meetings as productive and even enjoyable, and find out if there are any major problems. Some items you might discuss are:

- How are we doing, generally?
- How do you feel about the new home?
- How are the bedrooms working out?
- Do you have any suggestions?
- Are there some things that we should change, or that we should start doing?
- Are there some activities that we want to start doing together?

Children come up with wonderful suggestions. Listen carefully even to the youngest's ideas.

2. Get every child to speak.

Some children won't hesitate to speak up, but shy children may be tempted to hide. Don't let this dynamic get started. Everyone needs to participate and know that he or she is a valued, important member of the family whose suggestions are welcomed.

Begin with the rule that everyone gets to speak. On some questions, you may want to go around the room to make *sure* everyone says something. Draw each person out, no matter how young he or she is, and gently but firmly cut off the member who habitually hogs the stage.

3. No interrupting.

When someone is speaking, everyone else has to give that person his or her full attention—unless it becomes a filibuster. Being interrupted can be intimidating and can keep people from being involved the next time. Everyone has something valuable to say, if you take the time to listen. Even if what they say sounds like criticism, see if you can learn from it.

If someone seems to want to make trouble—interrupting, being hypercritical, cutting other people down—that person may just feel lost in the shuffle and need more time or attention. Offer what support you can—a shoulder to cry on, an ear to listen, therapy—but let him or her know that you won't let negative behavior ruin the meetings for everyone. If a few people develop alliances that exclude others or work against the group, talk to them and put a stop to it. Ask them what's going on and get them back into the group, even if they are critical.

4. Don't let it turn into a one-man/woman show.

If you find that you are the only one speaking, say, "Hey, I don't want to do this by myself. What's going on? What do you think?" You may want to put somebody on the spot by calling on him or her. Do this gently; don't force the person to speak if he or she is really not ready to do so, but don't let him or her off the hook immediately either.

5. Once a year, discuss what the past year has meant to each person and what each person's goals are for the future.

We did this at Christmas. It is a chance for everyone to get to know one another a little better, and to share some serious as well as some light moments. It gives everyone a chance to know what is really important to the other people in the family, and to learn how they can best support one another. Even when blended families don't live under the same roof, family meetings can be valuable. They bring people together to tell their individual truths, keep everyone up to date on what others are doing, thinking, and feeling, and can be a strong bonding experience.

ONE OF A KIND

Each blended family develops its own unique personality. You can't prescribe it, control it, or force it to be something it isn't. Believe me, no blended family will look like The Brady Bunch.

Each person brings his or her own expectations to the new family—both positive and negative—and not all these expectations will be met. The picture that emerges may contain elements of everyone's expectations, and also some that no one expected, but it probably won't follow anybody's blueprint exactly. Everyone will have to give a little.

You can say what you'd like it to be and influence it to some extent, but you have to accept your group as it is and realize that you can take them only so far on your shoulders. You can be responsible, build bridges, and start family meetings, but you have to let each family member participate as well. If you're doing it all and no one else is participating or doing his or her share, it's pointless.

This is a chance for everyone to develop better "people skills." Something will always come up in a blended family; each member according to his or her nature will learn how to cope, talk things out with one another, and come to solutions.

A blended family may be the ultimate expression of that Chinese character that stands for both "danger" and "opportunity." Use these exercises to lean that character toward "opportunity."

SUMMARY

- You are the source of leadership to your children.

- Your children will probably see the new person as an intruder.

- Present every situation as a positive opportunity or experience.

- Give everyone—especially yourself—plenty of room and forgiveness.

- Establish a clear structure of interaction among all the players and abide by it.

- The complexity of blended families is endless.

- When the two adults set the attitudes and behaviors, the children will follow.

◆

WORKBOOK EXERCISES

◆

1. Think of how your new partner has responded to your children and vice versa. How have you helped or hurt this process? List ways that you can encourage interaction between the new person in your life and your children.

2. Try to prepare the children ahead of time for any other changes that may occur. Make a list of changes you can anticipate.

3. With your new partner, set up a plan for blending the two families. Cover such issues as discipline, bedtimes, chores, allowances, etc.

4. Work out how, as a family, you will deal with the other extended family members. Include get-togethers, gifts, etc. (Make this part of the family forum.)

5. What are the areas that have caused trouble for you and other family members? Are they due to hangovers? Can they be resolved? If they are built into the new family, how can all of you come to terms with them?

Epilogue

◇

What the caterpillar calls the end of the world
the Master calls a butterfly.

—RICHARD BACH

◇

Each of you read this book with a specific goal in mind. For some of you, it was to understand the divorce process, complete it well, and avoid the hangover. For others, it was to recognize the hangover, discover how it grew out of the incomplete aspects of the divorce, pick up those "loose ends," and let go of the hangover.

You have come a long way and accomplished much. You have the means now to take hold of yourself and your life. Only you can be responsible for the direction that you want your life to take.

You have come to appreciate the importance of the decisions you make; you know that they can and will have consequences in your life from now on.

You have set forth a plan of action which, in the short run, will enable you to complete this phase of your life and to successfully disengage yourself from the past. In the long run, this plan will enable you to become whole and to have more fulfilling relationships.

Along the way, you have come to know and accept yourself more completely. You have trusted yourself to take risks—small or large—and this ability will grow if it is nurtured.

You have come to know that reality—good or bad—is all you have, and that your future depends on grasping what is *now* and then going forward with grace and humor. You know now that whatever the future holds, you are equipped to handle it. As you and the life around you change, you will be able to make the appropriate adjustments.

You understand better the nature of divorce and the role that it played or is playing in your life. You have known divorce intimately. It is time to relinquish it along with your former relationship. Divorce and its hangover are no longer your permanent state of mind or your daily preoccupation. Your present reality and the person you have become are all you need to carry you wherever you choose to go.

It is all up to you.

THE #1 *NEW YORK TIMES* BESTSELLER

GAIL SHEEHY

Author of the phenomenal bestseller *Passages*

menopause

THE SILENT PASSAGE

A MYTH-SHATTERING INVESTIGATION
OF AMERICA'S LAST TABOO:
MENOPAUSE

POCKET
BOOKS NOW AVAILABLE FROM POCKET BOOKS 867

Fascinating New Sexual Fantasies from the Bestselling Author of *My Secret Garden*

NANCY FRIDAY

HOW REAL LIFE HAS CHANGED WOMEN'S SEXUAL FANTASIES

WOMEN ON TOP

Available from

POCKET
B O O K S

621-01